The New
Practitioner's Guide

The New Practitioner's Guide To

CENTER
FOR URBAN
POLICY RESEARCH

Fiscal Impact Analysis

Robert W. Burchell
David Listokin
William R. Dolphin

Published in the United States of America
by the Center for Urban Policy Research
Building 4051—Kilmer Campus
New Brunswick, New Jersey 08903

The Practitioner's Guide to Fiscal Impact Analysis *was prepared under a grant from the U.S. Department of Housing and Urban Development, Office of Policy Development and Research, Product Dissemination and Transfer Division. It was field tested and evaluated at training sessions for local planners and financial analysts conducted in cooperation with the Commonwealth of Pennsylvania, Department of Community Affairs. Preparation of the report was directed by Gene Ritzenthaler of the Division of Product Dissemination and Transfer.*

The statements and conclusions contained herein are those of the authors and do not necessarily reflect the views of the U.S. Government in general or particularly the U.S. Department of Housing and Urban Development. Neither the Federal Government nor the Department of Housing and Urban Development makes any warranty, expressed or implied, or assumes responsibility for the accuracy or completeness of the information herein.

Library of Congress Cataloging in Publication Data

Burchell, Robert W.
  The new practitioner's guide to fiscal impact analysis.

  Rev. ed. of: Practitioner's guide to fiscal impact analysis/Robert W. Burchell, David Listokin, William R. Dolphin. c1980.
  1. Municipal services—Finance. 2. Real estate development—Costs. 3. Tax revenue estimating. I. Listokin, David. II. Burchell, Robert W. III. Dolphin, William R. Practitioner's guide to fiscal impact analysis. IV. Title.
HD4431.B856   1985   352.1   85-5944
ISBN 0-88285-109-8 (pbk.)

Contents

SECTION   *PAGE*

     PREFACE   ix

  I. INTRODUCTION AND DEFINITIONS   1

  II. FISCAL IMPACT COST PROJECTION METHODS   6

 III. FISCAL IMPACT REVENUE PROJECTION TECHNIQUES   39

 IV. RELATED INFORMATION TO FISCAL IMPACT ANALYSIS:
LEGAL, MODELS, MULTIPLIERS   50

  V. HYPOTHETICAL FISCAL IMPACT PROBLEMS AND
SOLUTIONS   54

 VI. UPDATED DEMOGRAPHIC MULTIPLIERS (STANDARD
HOUSING TYPES) *1980 U.S. CENSUS OF POPULATION AND
HOUSING*   62

Exhibits

EXHIBIT NUMBER   PAGE

1. EXAMPLE FISCAL IMPACT COST PROJECTION USING
   THE PER CAPITA MULTIPLIER METHOD   12

2a. REGIONAL AND NATIONAL DEMOGRAPHIC
    MULTIPLIERS (TOTAL HOUSEHOLD SIZE)   13

2b. REGIONAL AND NATIONAL DEMOGRAPHIC
    MULTIPLIERS (SCHOOL-AGE CHILDREN)   14

3. EXAMPLE FISCAL IMPACT COST PROJECTION
   USING THE CASE STUDY METHOD   18

4. EXAMPLE FISCAL IMPACT COST PROJECTION
   USING THE SERVICE STANDARD METHOD   21

5. SERVICE STANDARDS FOR FULL-TIME PUBLIC
   EMPLOYMENT (SOUTHERN REGION)   22

6. EXAMPLE FISCAL IMPACT COST PROJECTION
   USING THE COMPARABLE CITY METHOD   27

7. OPERATING EXPENDITURE MULTIPLIERS BY
   POPULATION SIZE AND GROWTH RATE   28

8. EXAMPLE FISCAL IMPACT COST PROJECTION
   USING THE PROPORTIONAL VALUATION METHOD   32

9. REFINEMENT COEFFICIENTS FOR THE PROPORTIONAL
   VALUATION METHOD   33

10. EXAMPLE FISCAL IMPACT COST PROJECTION
    USING THE EMPLOYMENT ANTICIPATION METHOD   37

11. EXPENDITURE MULTIPLIERS FOR THE EMPLOYMENT
    ANTICIPATION METHOD   38

12. 1980 DEMOGRAPHIC MULTIPLIERS—TOTAL
    HOUSEHOLD SIZE   64

13. 1980 DEMOGRAPHIC MULTIPLIERS—SCHOOL-AGE
    CHILDREN   65

14. 1980 DEMOGRAPHIC MULTIPLIERS—SCHOOL-AGE
    CHILDREN BY GRADE   66

15. 1980 DEMOGRAPHIC MULTIPLIERS—PERCENT OF
    SCHOOL-AGE CHILDREN IN PUBLIC SCHOOL   69

16. 1980 DEMOGRAPHIC MULTIPLIERS—PERCENT OF
    CHILDREN IN PUBLIC SCHOOL BY GRADE   70

17. 1980 DEMOGRAPHIC MULTIPLIERS—PRE-SCHOOL
    CHILDREN   73

Preface

The New Practitioner's Guide to Fiscal Impact Analysis is the third in a series of studies conducted by the Rutgers University Center for Urban Policy Research over the past decade. The first, *The Fiscal Impact Handbook,* presented detailed impact projection procedures and also provided the then most-current household size and school-age children data by type/size of housing unit—that available from the *1970 Census of Population and Housing*–Public Use Sample. The second study, the *Practitioner's Guide to Fiscal Impact Analysis,* summarized the fiscal impact techniques in an instructional format. It also updated the household and school-age children profiles by analyzing the most appropriate intercensal data base—the *American (Annual) Housing Survey.*

Both *The Fiscal Impact Handbook* and the *Practitioner's Guide to Fiscal Impact Analysis* have been adopted by planning bodies, planning professionals, demographers, students and others as a basic reference. They are applied in many contexts including comparing the costs and revenues of a proposed new development, analyzing the community-wide fiscal consequences of municipal land use policies, and conducting school enrollment projections.

The *Practitioner's Guide to Fiscal Impact Analysis* draws its sustenance and strength from *The Fiscal Impact Handbook*. The *Handbook* is also in its fourth printing and will undergo complete revision in 1986. Subsequent to the revision of the *Handbook* there will be a completely new edition of the *Practitioner's Guide.*

Pending a new edition of the *Practitioner's Guide,* it is imperative that the basic reference be kept as current as possible. This is especially critical with respect to the household and school-age children counts as these have changed with the changing demographic profile and housing consumption of the American family.

The New Practitioner's Guide to Fiscal Impact Analysis provides household size and school children multipliers from the most current and comprehensive available data source—the 1980 *Census of Population and Housing*–Public Use Sample. In response to the broadened application of *The Fiscal Impact Handbook* and *Practitioner's Guide* series, it presents an expanded range of demographic information. In addition to school-age multipliers, the current study indicates the share of the school-age population which attends the public schools (public school children multipliers) as well as the count of the pre-school-age population. The former is instructive for defining the public sector educational responsibility and financial obligation; the latter is important for determining future school load, whether in public or non-public schools.

In sum, *The New Practitioner's Guide to Fiscal Impact Analysis* makes available current demographic data and presents it in a format conducive to application in a wide variety of impact projections.

The New
Practitioner's Guide

I. INTRODUCTION AND DEFINITIONS

INTRODUCTION TO THE PRACTITIONER'S GUIDE AND TO FISCAL IMPACT ANALYSIS

Introduction to the Practitioner's Guide

The purpose of the *Practitioner's Guide* is to present a summary of fiscal impact analysis for instructional purposes.[1] It is designed to be used by experienced planners for the familiarization of entry level planners and lay public officials or planning board members with techniques and procedures to evaluate the public costs and revenues associated with development. The *Practitioner's Guide* is an administrator's tool for the teaching of fiscal impact analysis. Its contents have been carefully selected and arranged to provide only information essential for the successful completion of fiscal impact instruction.

---

1. The *Practitioner's Guide* is derived from a HUD funded research contract to assemble and disseminate standardized techniques to evaluate the public costs and revenues of land development. This study is available in two versions: The *Fiscal Impact Handbook,* published by the Rutgers University Center for Urban Policy Research, and The *Fiscal Impact Guidebook,* published by the U.S. Department of Housing and Urban Development and available from the Government Printing Office. The *Practitioner's Guide* summarizes the fiscal impact procedures contained in these studies, adds hypothetical problems for instructional purposes, and presents updated demographic multipliers. It is an ideal handout for individual or group instruction to be used with the *Handbook* or *Guidebook* as a basic reference.

The *Practitioner's Guide* is divided into six sections:

> I. *Introduction and Definitions*
> II. *Fiscal Impact Cost Projection Methods*
> III. *Fiscal Impact Revenue Projection Techniques*
> IV. *Related Information to Fiscal Impact Analysis:*
>   *Legal, Models, Multipliers*
> V. *Hypothetical Fiscal Impact Problems and Solutions*
> VI. *Updated Demographic Multipliers*

The *Introduction and Definitions* section discusses the organization of the *Guide* and carefully defines fiscal impact analysis.

Section II contains detailed *Cost Projection Methods.* For each method information is presented on: assumptions, advantages/disadvantages, and data requirements. This section also includes information on method applicability, i.e., which of the various methods should be employed given certain fiscal and problematical conditions at the site of the analysis.

In Section III, *Revenue Projection Techniques,* are found summaries of the revenues which are affected by growth as well as procedures for the calculation of potential revenue impacts. This is true for local revenues, i.e., taxes and charges, as well as for intergovernmental transfers from both the state and federal governments.

Section IV presents *Related Information* to fiscal impact analysis—how the procedure is used in ongoing planning, its legal standing, and the models and multipliers which may be used for its effectuation.

Section V contains *Hypothetical Problems and Solutions* which may be administered by the practitioners as working examples of each method.

Section VI presents *Updated Demographic Multipliers,* those derived for standard housing types using the *1980 U.S. Census of Population and Housing.*

Introduction to Fiscal Impact Analysis

The purpose of this *Guide* is to describe and demonstrate applications for the various techniques which have emerged to gauge the public costs of land development. These techniques are grouped under a common procedural description—*fiscal impact analysis.* All seek to predict both the municipal and educational servicing costs which accrue due to the public service demands of various forms of residential and nonresidential growth.

The technique, fiscal impact analysis, is not new—it is now close to fifty years old. Planners first employed this type of evaluation in the early public housing effort of the 1930's to justify the replacement of deteriorated structures due to their negative local fiscal effects. In the late 1940's it was used in the urban renewal movement to demonstrate the revenue generating superiority of the new land use that would replace the old. Since that time there has been steady growth in its employment through the 1950's, 1960's, into the 1970's. Fiscal impact analyses are now used to project the economic impact of alternative development proposals, major zoning or subdivision review plans, for boundary changes, municipal annexations, large scale, mixed-use developments or new communities, and as an integral part of the filing procedure for an environmental impact statement.

Today, there is a growing awareness that if it is possible to estimate the costs associated with growth, it may further be possible to dampen the short run service discontinuities usually associated with this growth and to allow the many public services which support development to be in-place and available when they are needed. There is, as a result, a growing *demand* for straightforward, standardized methods to estimate the local public costs and revenues associated with land development.

Yet what is the *current* state of the art? In an analysis of 140 cost-revenue studies obtained from around the country, it was clear that in the majority of cases their quality was poor. Twenty percent of the studies were either incomplete, could not be followed, or were conceptually or technically wrong. In over half the locations where the study was undertaken, the presiding local official could not gauge the study's accuracy. In 60 percent of the cases there was no way for technicians to use an existing fiscal impact analysis without the specific local consultants or staff planners who prepared the original report. This view of field practice indicated a pressing need for standardized methods, with explicit assumptions . . . and careful definitions as to the costs and revenues which were or were not being considered. Further, it was clear that there was now more than one fiscal impact method and sensitivity had to be paid to an appropriate pairing of method with task. This *Guide* is an attempt to answer these obvious field needs.

DEFINITION OF FISCAL IMPACT ANALYSIS

Fiscal impact analysis, as used here, is:

> *A projection of the direct, current, public costs and revenues associated with residential or nonresidential growth to the local jurisdiction(s) in which this growth is taking place.*

Certain terms in this definition must be clearly understood. The following paragraphs discuss them in detail.

Fiscal impact analysis, as explained in this *Guide,* considers *direct* impact. It projects only the primary costs that will be incurred and the immediate revenues that will be generated. Direct or primary costs include, for example, salaries for instructors to teach new students generated by a large subdivision, or for policemen to control traffic at a new shopping center. Direct or primary revenues include property and sales taxes and intergovernmental monies generated as a consequence of the specific growth increment. Indirect impacts are not treated due to: (1) the near impossibility of predicting accurately the secondary consequences of growth; and (2) the recurring potential for double counting when primary and secondary impacts are viewed simultaneously. In the first case, will a shopping center increase real property values of adjacent parcels or does the presence of an immediate market enhance the value of the shopping center? In the second, should property tax revenues from an off-site nonresidential development, which in part is supported by a residential development, be considered the primary impact of the nonresidential development or the secondary impact of the residential development? This *Guide* considers no differential property value loss or gain relative to proximate development due to property or sales tax increases of a nonresidential facility benefitting from the nearby population. In the first case, it is assumed that the "contagion effects" of land uses in the long run will net to zero. In the second, the revenue contributions of any land use are considered only when that land use's primary fiscal impact is under scrutiny.

Fiscal impact analysis examines *current* costs and revenues. It tallies the financial effects of a planned unit development, urban renewal complex, new town, shopping center, etc. by considering the costs and revenues such facilities would generate if they were completed and operating today. This approach recognizes that development or redevelopment often requires several years and that inflation will increase costs and revenues over time. It also assumes, however, that the rising costs of providing public services will be matched by an essentially comparable increase in revenues—that the relative relationship of costs and revenues will change little over time.

Fiscal impact analysis is concerned with *public* (governmental) costs and revenues. It does not consider private costs of public actions, i.e., the costs passed on to developers or consumers through local land use regulations or building, health, and fire codes. Thus, special assessments on real property or the value of land dedications required of developers are considered private revenues. Private services provided by home associations and community trusts are also considered private expenditures.

Tallying and comparing *costs and revenues* are significant parts of fiscal impact analysis. Costs include operating expenditures (salaries, statutory and material costs) and capital outlays, either directly incurred by a public jurisdiction or paid to others as a result of a specific development. Revenues comprise all monies a government receives from external sources as a result of the development or redevelopment. Revenues counted in a fiscal impact analysis include municipal and school district own source (local) contributions (taxes, charges, and miscellaneous revenue) and state and Federal intergovernmental transfers.

Fiscal impact analysis is further concerned with the cost and revenue implications derived from *population and/or employment change*. These changes are broadly defined as residential and/or nonresidential entrance into or departure from a community. The fiscal impact analysis may be a prediction or a post hoc evaluation and may evaluate population and/or employment change in either the private or public sectors (i.e., a builder attempting to develop a mixed use planned unit development or a local authority seeking municipal approval for a public housing project or a civic center).

Finally, costs are projected to only the *local jurisdictions* in which the population or employment change is taking place. In most instances, the local jurisdiction is the town, township, borough, or parish for municipal costs and the school district(s) for primary and secondary school district expenditures. Fiscal impact analysis, as defined here, does not consider services administered by and revenues flowing to utilities, special districts, county governments, regional authorities, and states.

Emphasizing projections of exclusively local costs reflects user demand. Local governments—either municipal or school district—provide most services to residential and nonresidential properties. Police and fire protection, road maintenance and repair, education, etc., represent types of local government services. Local property owners must often share the cost of these services. Impacts on the cost are of vital interest to the local population; fiscal impact analyses volunteered by developers or required by local ordinances are the result. Services provided by special districts are usually paid for with user charges. They typically do not affect the local population directly. County government services in areas where local governments also provide services to property frequently involve major road construction or repair and institution or agency maintenance. The effect of change in their expenditures (related to a particular growth increment) on local residents is usually relatively small and not of vital concern.

Practitioner's Notes

(1) Emphasize the underlined portion of the definition.

(2) Point out interchangeability of fiscal impact analysis and cost-revenue analysis yet differences between fiscal impact analysis and cost effective or cost benefit analysis.

(3) Make clear that a development's secondary impacts are *not* ignored. Rather they are analyzed when they appear as their own primary impacts.

(4) Underscore analysts' concern with *publicly* funded activities and *publicly* raised revenues.

II. COST PROJECTION METHODS

METHODS OF FISCAL IMPACT ANALYSIS AND THEIR APPLICATION

The Methods of Fiscal Impact Analysis

There are two basic approaches to municipal cost allocation: average costing and marginal costing. Average costing is by far the more common field application. Costs are attributed to a new development according to average cost per unit of service (municipal and school district services) times the number of units the development is estimated to require. This method does not consider existing excess or deficient capacity that might exist for particular services or the possibility that a new development might fall at the threshold level, calling for major new capital construction to accommodate increased growth. Both of these deficiencies could invalidate an average cost assumption. Marginal costing, however, takes both of these potential deficiencies into account. Marginal costing relies heavily on careful analysis of existing demand/supply relationships for local governmental and school services.

The average cost and marginal cost approaches are two different ways to assess the cost of governmental services that growth imposes. Average costing views the relationships as linear while marginal costing views growth as having a more cyclical impact on local expenditures. In the extremely long run, however, the two techniques will yield similar estimates of growth impact. The difference is that at times the marginal cost estimate will lag behind the average cost projection while in other instances the marginal cost estimate will lead or exceed the average cost figures. For example, marginal costs may be low in communities where unused facilities are available for an increased population; they are high when new facilities are to be built and new services provided that are greater than those immediately needed by the incoming population. Choosing either the average costing or marginal costing approaches will depend on what the fiscal impact analyst seeks—a best average estimate of the fiscal effects of growth, in which case the analyst will select the average costing approach, or a more intimate projection, in which case the analyst will opt for the marginal costing technique.

6

The *Guide* summarizes six different methods to analyze cost-revenue impact. They are relatively simple and straightforward in nature, based on the derivation of either average or marginal cost-revenue characteristics from recent municipal and school district budgetary data. It is assumed that the recent cost-revenue characteristics of individual land uses will be maintained in the future. Because of their simplicity, these fiscal impact analysis techniques do not represent forecasting "models" of the more rigorous type (typically based upon sophisticated statistical analysis or mathematical modeling); rather, they represent ad hoc analysis techniques for estimating the likely cost-revenue impact of different land-use development patterns, based upon recent historical expenditure experience in the specific locality or in a suitably chosen likeness of that locality.

Three of the six fiscal impact analysis techniques—Per Capita Multiplier, Service Standard, and Proportional Valuation—represent average costing approaches, while the three remaining techniques—Case Study, Comparable City and Employment Anticipation—represent marginal costing strategies.

All but two of the six methods—Proportional Valuation and Employment Anticipation—are used for estimating the impacts of residential activity. The remaining two are applicable for nonresidential land uses, while the Case Study is used for both residential and nonresidential projections. Since the same methods for revenue estimation may be utilized under any technique, emphasis is given to differences in the estimation of public service costs.

Method Application

Fiscal impact methods are applied to fiscal impact tasks based on: *(1) fiscal conditions at the site of the analysis and (2) the type of problem with which the analyst is faced.* In the first case, is the city's public service delivery system in tune with demand or is it drastically over- or under-utilized? If the services the city supplies are reasonably close to the level of demand that is being experienced, the assumption can be made that future costs are a reflection of current costs, and average costing methods (Per Capita Multiplier, Service Standard, Proportional Valuation) can be employed. If, on the other hand, excess or deficient service capacity exists, the marginal strategies (Case Study, Comparable City, Employment Anticipation) should be used.

In the second case (type of problem), if the analyst is faced with a small development proposal or several development alternatives, the simpler, usually average costing approaches, should be used. A large or unique development proposal will usually require one of the marginal costing methods.

Using these two primary sorting procedures, methods may be applied, generally speaking, as indicated in the chart on the following page. For large, declining cities or small rapid growth suburbs, the Case Study Method is almost always appropriate for large complex developments and even for smaller developments or development alternatives. For mid-size, moderate growth suburbs, the Per Capita Multiplier Method is appropriate for smaller developments or alternative development scenarios whereas the Service Standard Method is more appropriate for the large, single development case.

For nonresidential impact analyses, the Case Study Method should be used in large, declining cities or small, rapid-growth areas. The Proportional Valuation Method is almost always employed in mid-size, moderate growth communities, especially in situations where only a rough gauge of impact is desired.

FISCAL IMPACT METHOD APPLICATIONS

Status of Community's Existing ROW Service Capacity	Community Most Typifying Service Capacity	Development Proposals (Residential)	Development Proposals (Nonresidential)	Land Use Alternatives	Rezoning/ Variances	Annexations/ Boundary Changes	EIS's	Urban Renewal/ Community Redevelopment
1. Significant excess capacity[a]	Central city—declining moderately or slightly	CS	CS	CS/CC	CS/CC	CS	CS	CS
2. At capacity,[b] slight excess capacity	Second order city—stable growth or declining slightly	CS/CC	CS/EA	CS/CC	CS/CC	CS	CS/CC	CS
3. At capacity	Suburb—stable growth or slightly increasing	M/SS	PV/EA	M/SS	M/SS	M/SS	M/SS	CS
4. At capacity, slight deficient capacity[c]	Suburb-moderately increasing growth	M/SS	PV/EA	M/SS	M/SS	M/SS	M/SS	
5. Moderate deficient capacity	Exurban—moderately increasing growth	CS/CC	CS	CS/CC	CS/CC	M/SS	CS/CC	
6. Significant deficient capacity	Exurban—rapidly increasing growth	CS/CC	CS	CS	CS/CC	CS	CS	

Notes:

a. *Excess Capacity*—This service system is underutilized and exhibits room for service expansion without significant additional operational or capital expenditures.

b. *At Capacity*—The service system is operating at its most efficient level; most service categories exhibit neither over nor underutilization.

c. *Deficient Capacity*—The service system is overutilized; the slightest form of additional service demand will occasion significant operational or capital expenditures.

Applicable Methods: M = Per Capita Multiplier
CS = Case Study
SS = Service Standard
CC = Comparable City
PV = Proportional Valuation
EA = Employment Anticipation

Practitioner's Notes

(1) Emphasize that in some fiscal impact problems *multiple* methods may be used.
(2) In borderline situations (fiscal conditions at impact site may not provide clear insight as to which method to use) two or more methods may be employed as a check against the accuracy of any one method

PER CAPITA MULTIPLIER METHOD

Background

The Per Capita Multiplier Method is the classic average costing approach for projecting the impact of population change on local municipal and school district costs and revenues. Due to its simplicity and ease of operation, the method has been applied to almost every type of fiscal impact situation.

The Per Capita Multiplier Method relies on detailed demographic information by housing type (total household size and number of school-age children) and the average cost, per person and per pupil, of municipal and school district operating expenses (including the amortization of capital expenditures) to project an annual (operating/ capital) cost assignable to a particular population change. Using the Proportional Valuation Method, the technique begins by sifting off the local costs assigned to nonresidential uses. Then it expresses all local municipal costs per person and school district costs per pupil. These per capita and per pupil costs, multiplied by an estimate of the population shift resulting from growth (partitioned by pupils and adults) are the incremental costs assigned to the specific growth generator.

To illustrate, assume that a midwestern municipality is attempting to analyze the local fiscal impact of 100 garden apartments (80 percent-one bedroom, 20 percent-two bedroom). Units in the proposed development will probably rent for an average of $250 and $300 monthly and are estimated to be valued at $15,000 and $21,000 per unit, respectively. Demographic profiles of garden apartments for the area indicate that an average 1.686 residents and 0.036 school-age children may be expected to reside in one bedroom units and 2.685 residents and 0.232 school-age children in two bedroom units. Information obtained from the city manager and superintendent of schools tabulates current total municipal operating costs per person at $250 annually and total school district costs per pupil at $1,500 annually. The development is assigned $33,720 (80 units x 1.686 persons per unit x $250 per person) in municipal costs and $4,320 (80 units x 0.036 children per unit x $1,500 per child) in school district costs for the local fiscal impact of one-bedroom units, and $13,425 in municipal costs (20 x 2.685 x $250), and $6,960 in school district costs (20 x 0.232 x $1,500) for two-bedroom units. The total cost to the municipality and school district for operations and capital additions for the 100 unit garden apartment development is thus estimated at approximately $58,000 annually ($33,720 + $4,320 + $13,425 + $6,960).

Assumptions

A basic assumption of the Per Capita Multiplier Method is that over the long run, *current* average operating costs per capita and per student are the best estimates of *future* operating costs occasioned by growth. A second assumption is that current *local* service levels are the most accurate indicators of future service levels and that they will continue on the same scale in the future. A further premise is that the current composition of the population occasioning costs and the population contributing to future costs are sufficiently similar that the above scenario will remain unaltered.

A fourth and final premise is that the current distribution of expenditures among the various sectors of municipal service will remain constant in the short run and will serve as the primary indicator of the way in which additional expenditures will be subsequently allocated.

Procedures & Example Calculation

See pp. 11-12

Advantages & Disadvantages

Advantages

Simplicity/Low Cost The Per Capita Multiplier Method is similar to the Comparable City and Service Standard Methods in terms of ease of implementation.

Acceptability The Per Capita Multiplier Method is the most widely accepted fiscal impact procedure available, particularly for the private planning consultant.

Disadvantages

Richness of Detail Probably the single greatest disadvantage of this method is the detail to which results are available. Its most accurate indication of costs is only to the level of municipal and school district services.

Practitioner's Notes

(1) Emphasize that this is the most versatile, easily understood, simple to implement and thus, widely employed method.
(2) Assumption that current costs per unit are the best indication of future costs is key to method.
(3) Heed strengths and weaknesses of demographic multipliers as detailed in Chapter 13 of the *Handbook/Guidebook*.
(4) Make point that method is inherently site influenced—all information is obtained from historical local expenditure patterns.

PER CAPITA MULTIPLIER FISCAL IMPACT METHOD: SUMMARY OF COST PROJECTION PROCEDURES

STEP NUMBER	ANALYSIS/ACTIONS	EXAMPLE CALCULATION (A 3,000 UNIT PUD IS PROPOSED FOR A N.J. COMMUNITY OF 16,000 POPULATION. SEE EXHIBIT 1 FOR FULL COST PROJECTION.)
1	Contact the office of the city manager and superintendent of schools to obtain local municipal and school district budgets and the latest estimates of municipal/school district populations.	This step reveals the following local information: Municipal population of 16,000 residents; Total municipal expenditures of $3,266,171; School district population of 2,400 pupils; and educational expenditures of $4,440,000
2	Categorize local expenditures into five municipal service categories plus the school district function.	Step 2 disaggregates total local municipal and school district expenditures into component services—general government, public safety, public works, health and welfare, recreation and culture and school district.
3	Obtain total annual municipal expenditures by summing the annual costs, including debt service for capital facilities, for each of the five service categories. Obtain total annual school district expenditures.	Step 3 aggregates component service costs into total municipal and total school district outlays.
4	Assign a share of total annual municipal costs to existing local nonresidential facilities based on the proportion of their value to total local real property valuation. Subtract this share from the total annual municipal costs.	The Proportional Valuation Method (see Exhibit 8) is used to determine local, nonresidential induced municipal expenditures in the example community. This amount ($1,199,338) is subtracted from total local municipal costs ($3,266,171) to yield residential induced expenditures of $2,066,833 ($3,266,171 - $1,199,338).
5	Calculate the net (residentially-induced) annual costs of the five municipal functions on a per capita basis and the annual costs of education on a per pupil basis.	$$\text{Municipal Costs Per Capita} = \frac{\text{Residential Induced Expenditures}}{\text{Total Municipal Population}}$$ $$= \frac{\$2,066,833}{16,000}$$ $$\$129$$ $$\text{Per Pupil Education Costs} = \frac{\text{Total Educational Expenditures}}{\text{Total School District Pupils}}$$ $$= \frac{\$4,400,000}{2,400}$$ $$\$1,850$$
6	Calculate anticipated total resident and school population by housing type.	As example community is in New Jersey,* use demographic multipliers for Northeast region, Middle Atlantic subregion (see Exhibit 2 and Exhibit 1, column 2). See Exhibit 1 columns 1-3 for calculation of total resident (8,154) and school (1,456) populations.
7	Calculate residentially-induced total annual municipal and school district expenditure increases by multiplying per capita/per pupil municipal and school district expenditures by the projected number of residents/pupils.	See Exhibit 1, columns 3-5 for calculation. This step indicates that the PUD's residential component will generate $3,342,166 in local expenditures.
8	Calculate municipal costs for any nonresidential uses if they are inclusive of the growth increment; assign a share of local costs to the nonresidential facility based on the facility's share of total local nonresidential property valuation.	The Proportional Valuation Method indicates that the PUD's nonresidential component will generate $12,353 in local municipal costs. The PUD therefore increases total local costs by $3,354,519 ($3,342,166 + $12,353).
9	Determine total annual public costs and refine the projection by allocating total costs by service category.	The PUD generated total costs of $3,354,519 is disaggregated into the different public service components following the percentage breakdowns determined in Step 2.

*See page 57 for distribution of 50 states by region and subregion. Reference this page in selecting the appropriate demographic multipliers.

EXHIBIT 1

EXAMPLE FISCAL IMPACT COST PROJECTION USING THE PER CAPITA MULTIPLIER METHOD

USING THE PER CAPITA MULTIPLIER METHOD TO EVALUATE THE FISCAL IMPACT OF A DEVELOPMENT PROPOSAL

3,000 Unit Planned Unit Development	Number of Dwelling Units (1)	Demographic Multipliers Household/Students (2)		Total Residents[1] / Students[1] (3)		Annual Expenditure Per Capita/Municipal[2] / Annual Expenditure Per Pupil/School District[2] (4)		Total Annual Expenditures/Municipal[4] / Total Annual Expenditures/School District[4] (5)		Total Annual Public (Municipal and School District) Expenditures (6)
RESIDENTIAL										
Townhouses (1,500)										
1 bedroom (elderly)	250	1.699	0.000	425	—	$129	$1,850	$ 54,825	$ —	$ 54,825
2 bedroom	1,000	2.630	0.304	2,630	304	129	1,850	339,270	562,400	901,670
3 bedroom	250	4.110	1.311	1,028	328	129	1,850	132,612	606,800	739,412
Garden Apartments (1,000)										
1 bedroom	700	1.722	.011	1,205	8	129	1,850	155,445	14,800	170,245
2 bedroom	300	2.545	.200	758	60	129	1,850	97,782	111,000	208,782
Single-Family Homes (500)										
3 bedroom	250	3.776	1.111	944	278	129	1,850	121,776	514,300	636,076
4 bedroom	250	4.655	1.911	1,164	478	129	1,850	150,156	884,300	1,034,456
Total Residential	3,000	—	—	8,154	1,238 (1,456)[3]	—	—	1,051,866	2,290,300[5] (2,693,600)[6]	3,342,166[7] (3,745,466)[8]
NONRESIDENTIAL										
Community Shopping Center (100,000 Ft²)		—	—	—	—	—	—	12,353	—	12,353
TOTALS	3,000 (100,000 Ft²)			8,154	1,456	—	—	$1,064,219	$2,290,300	$3,354,519

Notes:

1 Equals the demographic multipliers shown in column (2) multiplied by the number of units shown in column (1).

2 Includes operating and debt service for capital facilities.

3 The figure in parenthesis is the actual subtotal of column (3) for projected pupils. Since the multipliers in column (2) are total school-age children rather than public school-age children and in this particular locale 15 percent of school-age children attend public schools, projected local pupils has been multiplied by 85 percent to reflect the actual anticipated public school burden.

4 Equals total residents/students multiplied by cost per resident/student.

5 Equals total *public* school-age children (1,238) multiplied by the cost per pupil ($1,850). This is the figure the analyst is interested in because it indicates actual generated **public costs.**

6 Equals total school-age children (1,456) multiplied by the cost per pupil ($1,850). It is also equal to the sum of the shown subtotals.

7 Equals $1,051,866 + $2,290,300.

8 Equals $1,051,866 + $2,693,600.

EXHIBIT 2A

REGIONAL AND NATIONAL DEMOGRAPHIC MULTIPLIERS
(TOTAL HOUSEHOLD SIZE)

REGIONAL AND NATIONAL DEMOGRAPHIC MULTIPLIERS FOR COMMON CONFIGURATIONS OF STANDARD HOUSING TYPES [1]
TOTAL HOUSEHOLD SIZE BY HOUSING TYPE AND SIZE
(U.S. CENSUS PUBLIC USE SAMPLE—1970)

HOUSING TYPES

	SINGLE FAMILY				GARDEN APARTMENTS			HIGH RISE				TOWN HOUSES				MOBILE HOMES			
	Two Bedroom	Three Bedroom	Four Bedroom	Blended	One Bedroom	Two Bedroom	Blended	Studio Bedroom	One Bedroom	Two Bedroom	Blended	One Bedroom	Two Bedroom	Three Bedroom	Blended	One Bedroom	Two Bedroom	Three Bedroom	Blended
REGION																			
NORTHEAST																			
New England	2.485	3.940	4.965	3.931	1.500	2.430	2.114	1.071	1.470	2.270	1.700	—	2.200	—[2]	—	—	2.390	3.588	2.595
Middle Atlantic	2.536	3.776	4.655	3.831	1.722	2.525	2.190	1.077	1.436	2.523	1.790	1.885	2.630	4.110	3.933	1.556	2.441	3.928	2.700
NORTH CENTRAL																			
East North Central	2.595	3.892	4.909	3.911	1.719	2.576	2.285	1.070	1.432	2.570	2.357	1.364	2.727	4.129	3.588	1.647	2.450	3.835	2.620
West North Central	2.517	3.714	4.840	3.697	1.584	2.479	2.195	—	1.386	—	1.515	—	2.833	3.500	3.015	1.757	2.402	3.877	2.654
SOUTH																			
South Atlantic	2.960	3.819	4.485	3.775	1.686	2.685	2.632	—	1.208	—	1.417	—	2.778	—	—	1.955	2.560	3.680	2.807
East South Central	2.823	3.683	4.550	3.608	1.576	2.622	2.418	—	1.367	2.385	1.619	—	2.600	4.000	2.844	2.065	2.697	3.793	2.910
West South Central	2.995	3.758	4.680	3.754	1.690	2.652	2.246	—	1.282	1.867	1.483	1.783	2.720	3.735	2.741	2.070	2.592	4.089	2.951
WEST																			
Mountain	2.865	3.716	4.486	3.983	1.667	2.570	2.216	1.050	1.333	2.000	1.443	—	2.154	—	—	1.739	2.551	4.013	2.960
Pacific	2.745	3.687	4.561	3.826	1.596	2.530	2.149	1.159	1.338	2.220	1.585	1.768	2.735	4.033	2.965	1.746	2.133	3.807	2.113
NATIONAL																			
(All Area Average)	2.673	3.752	4.665	—	1.653	2.560	—	1.112	1.435	2.270	—	1.859	2.731	4.073	—	1.754	2.431	3.865	—

See Section VI for updated demographic multipliers

Notes: 1 Units built from 1960-1970.
         2 Less than 1,000 units in this category (insufficient sample size).

Source: U.S. Census Public Use Sample, 1970.

EXHIBIT 2B

REGIONAL AND NATIONAL DEMOGRAPHIC MULTIPLIERS
(TOTAL SCHOOL-AGE CHILDREN SIZE)

REGIONAL AND NATIONAL DEMOGRAPHIC MULTIPLIERS FOR COMMON CONFIGURATIONS OF STANDARD HOUSING TYPES [1]
SCHOOL-AGE CHILDREN BY HOUSING TYPE AND SIZE
(U.S. CENSUS PUBLIC USE SAMPLE—1970)

HOUSING TYPES

REGION	SINGLE FAMILY				GARDEN APARTMENTS			HIGH RISE				TOWN HOUSES				MOBILE HOMES			
	Two Bedroom	Three Bedroom	Four Bedroom	Blended	One Bedroom	Two Bedroom	Blended	Studio	One Bedroom	Two Bedroom	Blended	One Bedroom	Two Bedroom	Three Bedroom	Blended	One Bedroom	Two Bedroom	Three Bedroom	Blended
NORTHEAST																			
New England	0.246	1.130	2.068	1.212	0.038	0.150	0.174	0.000	0.015	0.081	0.033	—	0.000	—[2]	0.640	—	0.268	0.324	0.396
Middle Atlantic	0.288	1.111	1.911	1.211	0.011	0.200	0.156	0.000	0.015	0.318	0.125	0.115	0.304	1.311	1.187	0.048	0.177	1.022	0.375
NORTH CENTRAL																			
East North Central	0.355	1.173	2.102	1.249	0.036	0.232	0.219	0.000	0.013	0.290	0.483	0.000	0.409	1.371	1.078	0.078	0.208	1.148	0.360
West North Central	0.361	1.099	2.063	1.142	0.023	0.165	0.173	0.000	0.068	—	0.136	—	0.389	0.750	0.544	0.135	0.233	1.169	0.430
SOUTH																			
South Atlantic	0.553	1.121	1.760	1.130	0.009	0.269	0.358	—	0.000	—	0.083	—	0.556	—	0.838	0.136	0.194	0.906	0.367
East South Central	0.443	1.066	1.728	1.024	0.035	0.306	0.323	—	0.000	—	0.021	0.000	0.267	1.500	0.656	0.323	0.262	0.928	0.422
West South Central	0.604	1.109	1.988	1.161	0.052	0.298	0.274	—	0.000	0.200	0.050	0.087	0.400	1.265	0.570	0.239	0.239	1.207	0.513
WEST																			
Mountain	0.404	1.081	1.825	1.364	0.034	0.246	0.245	0.000	0.000	0.000	0.000	—	0.231	—	0.577	0.043	0.283	1.158	0.565
Pacific	0.445	1.106	1.842	1.255	0.040	0.307	0.290	0.023	0.000	0.098	0.069	0.015	0.322	1.333	0.617	0.031	0.159	1.433	0.192
NATIONAL (All Area Average)	0.401	1.104	1.924	—	0.043	0.271	—	0.012	0.017	0.182	—	0.103	0.345	1.331	—	0.074	0.207	1.076	—

See Section VI for updated demographic multipliers

Notes: 1   Units built from 1960-1970.
             2   Less than 1,000 units in this category (insufficient sample size).

Source: U.S. Census Public Use Sample, 1970.

CASE STUDY METHOD

Background

The Case Study Method is the classic marginal cost approach to project the effect of population change on municipal and school district costs.

The Case Study Method employs intensive site-specific investigations to determine categories of *excess* or slack public service capacity (capacity beyond that needed to accommodate the existing service or target population at current public service levels) or *deficient* or overage capacity (capacity below that needed to accommodate the existing service or target population). The excess or deficient service capacities are subtracted from or added to best estimates of the operating and capital demands posed by growth for each service category. (Estimated changes in service population is the measure by which public officials gauge future operating and capital reactions.) The result of population-imposed need, mitigated by existing excess capacity or worsened by deficient capacity, is projected future public response for each service category.

For example, during an interview, the superintendent of schools reveals that both number of students per classroom and pupil-teacher ratios are significantly lower than in the past. He estimates that constructing a housing development will cause classroom size and pupil-teacher ratios to increase to previous levels but will not require new teachers to be hired or capital facilities to be expanded. In this case of obvious excess capacity, the new development is charged a minimal cost. In another example, however, new development requires that a rescue station must immediately be built, and additional firemen hired to serve an area already partially developed. In the case of existing deficient capacity, the new development is charged the *full* extent of these additional expenditures, even though previous development has contributed to the cost and will benefit from both the new facility and the additional personnel.

Assumptions

The Case Study approach is based on four assumptions. The first assumption is that communities differ in the degree to which they exhibit excess or deficient service capacity which significantly affects the level of local service extensions. The second assumption is that marginal changes in providing municipal and school district services, as a reaction to excess or deficient service capacity, are the most accurate indications of future local servicing costs.

The third premise is that while current local service levels may be altered slightly, they, and not national standards, represent the criteria against which local excess and deficient capacity are calculated. The fourth and final assumption is that local department heads, intimately familiar with the service delivery capacity of their departments, provide the most accurate gauge of future expenditure extensions in a particular category of municipal or school district service.

Data Requirements

The basic data needed to implement the method—estimates of excess or deficient service capacity and expected local service responses—come from estimates made by local municipal employees. These factors are specific to each locality; they must be obtained through on-site interviews.

Procedures and Example Calculations

See pp. 17-18

Advantages and Disadvantages

Advantages

Richness of Detail The other fiscal impact analysis methods omit the detailing of manpower and capital facility needs as a prerequisite for assigning costs. The Case Study Method, however, not only predicts the financial consequences of growth, but also assigns the costs of growth to operating and capital facilities by component service category.

Disadvantages

Time and Cost The Case Study Method is complex and costly. The method requires extensive interviews and other field work. It is more expensive than the other fiscal impact analysis methods described in the *Guidebook*. The relative ease and simplicity of most other methods stand in contrast to the considerable time and cost necessary to undertake the Case Study Method.

Practitioner's Notes

(1) Emphasize the time consuming and, as such, costly aspects of this method to implement.
(2) Municipal officials' estimates may not always be accurate—use as an accuracy check, the Service Standard Method.
(3) Existing service excess or deficient capacity per municipal department will be the most difficult information to secure.
(4) There is no better method to employ for detailed results and intimate knowledge about the fiscal impact site.
(5) Municipal officials are often excellent sources of information for the distribution of service resources between residential and nonresidential uses.

SERVICE STANDARD METHOD

Background

The Service Standard Method is an average costing method which uses averages of manpower and capital facility service levels, obtained from the U.S. Census of Governments, for municipalities and school districts of similar size and geographic location. The Service Standard Method determines the total number of additional employees by service function (financial administration, general control, police, fire, highways, sewerage, sanitation, water supply, parks and recreation, and libraries) that will be required as the result of growth. The analyst determines the local operating cost for additional personnel adding local operating outlays (salary, statutory and equipment expenditures) per employee by service function (e.g., $14,500 per policeman, $13,900 per fireman) to an annual expenditure for capital facilities specific to the service function. The annual

CASE STUDY FISCAL IMPACT METHOD: SUMMARY OF COST PROJECTION PROCEDURES

EXAMPLE CALCULATION (A 3,000 UNIT PUD IS PROPOSED IN AN ILLINOIS COMMUNITY. ILLUSTRATIVE CALCULATIONS ARE FOR POLICE COSTS ONLY. SEE EXHIBIT 3 FOR ALL CALCULATIONS FOR PUBLIC SERVICES)

STEP NUMBER	ANALYSIS/ACTIONS	EXAMPLE CALCULATION
1	Contact "key" public officials, e.g., city manager, municipal administrator, superintendent of schools.	
2	Categorize public service functions and delineate responsibilities by local municipal and school district services.	Use Census of Governments' service categories to group local expenditure categories. Police protection is classified as follows:
3	Determine presence or absence, and magnitude of any existing public operating and capital excess or deficient capacity for various public services.	Interview local officials to determine existing slack or excess capacity in local services. The example community has the following police operating status (see Exhibit 3, Column 2 for status of other public services).
4	Project population and student increases through the use of appropriate multipliers. Estimate population-induced service demand, using primarily service standards and capital ratios.	As the example community is in Illinois, use demographic multipliers for North Central region and East North Central subregion. These multipliers yield a total project resident population of 8,360 residents. This population estimate, multiplied by appropriate service standards, gives an estimate of the project population-induced demand. For example, the service standard for policemen in North Central communities of 10,000 to 25,000 population is 1.72 police per 1,000 residents. Consequently, a PUD of 8,360 residents will necessitate 14 (8.360 x 1.72) policemen (see Exhibit 3, Column 3 for calculations for other public services).
5	Interview local public officials to determine how their respective departments will respond to growth (given identified areas of existing service excess or deficiency and the rough gauge of population-induced demand) in terms of expanding or not expanding their operating and capital capacities.	Police officials in the example community estimate that the PUD will require the hiring of 16 patrolmen (see Exhibit 3, Column 4 for calculations for other public services).
6	Project the costs that will be incurred by different public jurisdictions as a consequence of the manpower and facility expansions pinpointed in step 5.	As the average cost per patrolman in the Illinois community is $16,100 and the PUD requires the hiring of 16 patrolmen, the PUD generates public safety operating costs of $257,600 ($16,000 x 16; see Exhibit 3, Column 6 for calculations for other services).

Step 2 detail:

Census of Governments Service Category	Typical Line - Item Budget Classification
PUBLIC SAFETY Police Protection:	Department/Division/Office of: Police, Traffic Control and Maintenance

Step 3 detail:

Governmental Functions	Capacity Determination Excess	Deficient
PUBLIC SAFETY Police Protection:	+1 Dispatcher	-2 Patrolmen

Step 5 detail:

Governmental Functions	Local Service Response
PUBLIC SAFETY Police Protection:	16 Patrolmen

EXHIBIT 3

EXAMPLE FISCAL IMPACT COST PROJECTION USING THE CASE STUDY METHOD

USING THE CASE STUDY METHOD TO EVALUATE THE OPERATING FISCAL IMPACT OF A DEVELOPMENT PROPOSAL

Step 2 Government Functions (1)	Step 3 Capacity Determination Excess[1]	Step 3 Deficient[1] (2)	Step 4 Population-Induced Demand[2] (Employees) (3)	Step 5 Local Service Response (4)	Step 6 Local Operating Service Cost per Unit[3] (5)	Step 6 Cost of Local Response[4] (6)
MUNICIPAL						
GENERAL GOVERNMENT						
FINANCIAL & ADMINISTRATIVE	+1 Accountant	−1 Clerk	2.5	5 Clerks	$ 9,800	$ 49,000
GENERAL CONTROL/PUBLIC BUILDINGS	+2 Engineers	−2 Custodians	4.8	4 Custodians/3 Clerks	9,100/9,400	64,600
PUBLIC SAFETY						
POLICE PROTECTION	+1 Dispatcher	−2 Patrolmen	14.4	16 Patrolmen	16,100	257,600
FIRE PROTECTION	+1 Lieutenant	−1 Fireman	7.8	8 Firemen	15,900	127,200
HOUSING & URBAN RENEWAL	+2 Planners	−2 Secretaries	5.0	5 Laborers	8,000	40,000
PUBLIC WORKS						
HIGHWAYS	+1 Traffic Engineer	−1 Laborer	6.8	10 Laborers/5 Clerks	10,100/5,901	130,505
SEWERAGE	+1 Chemist	−1 Engineer	3.3	4 Engineers	16,900	67,600
SANITATION	+1 Supervisor	−2 San. Workers	3.5	4 San. Workers	15,100	60,400
WATER SUPPLY	+1 Engineer	−3 Technicians	4.7	2 Technicians	13,000	26,000
HEALTH AND WELFARE						
PUBLIC WELFARE	+1 Case Worker	−1 Clerk	6.0	8 Clerks	8,800	70,400
HOSPITALS	+1 Supervisor	−4 Orderlies	6.2	7 Orderlies	8,100	56,700
HEALTH	+1 Orderly	−1 Nurse	3.0	1 Nurse	12,495	12,495
	+1 Sanitary Aide					
RECREATION AND CULTURE						
PARKS AND RECREATION	+1 Supervisor	−1 Rec. Spec.	2.6	6 Rec. Specialists	8,000	48,000
LIBRARIES	+1 Clerk	−1 Librarian	1.3	2 Librarians/4 Clerks	10,000/9,000	56,000
	TOTAL +17	TOTAL −23	TOTAL 71.9 MUNICIPAL	TOTAL 94		
TOTAL MUNICIPAL OPERATING EXPENDITURES						1,066,500
SCHOOL DISTRICT						
LOCAL PRIMARY & SECONDARY	+7 Teachers	−2 Reading Spec.		70 Teachers	15,700	1,099,000
	+2 Supervisors	−1 A-V Aide		4 Reading Spec.	15,900	63,600
	+1 Librarian	−2 Clerks		3 A-V Aides	13,800	41,400
SCHOOL DISTRICT				8 Clerks	10,500	84,000
				15 Aides	8,900	133,500
				5 Administrators	18,400	92,000
				20 Other Personnel	9,000	180,000
	TOTAL +10	TOTAL −5	TOTAL SCHOOL DISTRICT 106.2 employees	TOTAL 125		
TOTAL SCHOOL DISTRICT OPERATING EXPENDITURES						1,693,500
TOTAL MUNICIPAL AND SCHOOL DISTRICT OPERATING EXPENDITURES						2,760,000

Notes: 1 A plus (+) indicates excess capacity while a minus (−) indicates deficient capacity.
2 Development-generated population and public school age children multiplied by the service standards.
3 Includes salaries, statutory expenditures and material costs per employee
4 Equals column 4 multiplied by column 5.

capital expenditure is obtained through the use of capital-to-operating service ratios derived from Census information, and applied to the local total operating cost per employee.

To illustrate, a Northeastern city of 33,000 residents will grow to 38,000 as a result of a new 1,600-unit single-family subdivision. Using service ratios of 2.33 policemen and 1.88 firemen per 1,000 population (for Northeastern municipalities of 25,000-49,999), if the community follows average service patterns specific to its population size and location a service demand for 11.7 policemen (2.33 x 5.0) and 9.4 firemen (1.88 x 5.0) will be created locally as a result of the development. At the previously stated local average operating cost per policeman ($14,500) and fireman ($13,900), the operating cost assignable to the development for just these two functional areas is $300,310 ($169,650 [$14,500 x 11.7] + $130,660 [$13,900 x 9.4]). Using a 0.025 capital-to-operating ratio (Northeastern municipalities of 25,000-49,999 population) for police capital expenditures and applying this to the product of the number of policemen to be added locally, the average local operations cost per policeman will add $4,241 ($169,650 x 0.025); a 0.005 capital-to-operations ratio for fire protection capital expenditures, similarly applied to the product of the additional firemen, and the average local operations cost per fireman will add an additional $653 ($130,660 x 0.005). The total assignable cost (operating plus capital debt service) to the growth increment for these two functions is $305,204. This procedure is repeated for each functional area listed above to ascertain total costs assignable.

Assumptions

A fundamental assumption of the Service Standard approach is that, over the long run average *existing* service levels for both manpower and capital facilities of comparable cities can be used to assign costs to future development.

Another premise of the technique is that service levels for both manpower and capital facilities vary according to the community's population. A further assumption is that after population size, geographic location also affects public service levels.

Data Requirements

The basic data needed to implement the Service Standard Method consist of multipliers for household size and school-age population for different types of housing; population estimates for municipalities and school districts; public employee service standards by service category; average operating costs per employee; and annual capital-to-operating expenditure ratios by service category.

Procedures and Example Calculation

See pp. 20-21

SERVICE STANDARD FISCAL IMPACT METHOD: SUMMARY OF COST PROJECTION PROCEDURES

EXAMPLE CALCULATION (A 2,000 UNIT SINGLE-FAMILY DEVELOPMENT IS PROPOSED FOR A GEORGIA COMMUNITY OF 16,000 POPULATION. ILLUSTRATIVE CALCULATIONS ARE FOR POLICE SERVICES ONLY. SEE EXHIBIT 4 FOR CALCULATIONS FOR ALL PUBLIC SERVICES.)

STEP NUMBER	ANALYSIS/ACTIONS	EXAMPLE CALCULATION
1	Using general multipliers for household and school age children, determine population and student increase resulting from growth.	As example community is in Georgia, use demographic multipliers for Southern region, South Atlantic subregion.

Number/type Housing	Household Size Multiplier	School-Age Children Multiplier	Total Residents	Total School-Age Children
2,000 single-family homes	3.775	1.130	7,550	2,260 (school-age children) 1,989 (Public school-age children)

STEP NUMBER	ANALYSIS/ACTIONS	EXAMPLE CALCULATION
2	Using service ratios for communities of different regions and sizes, project number of incremental public employees resulting from growth.	As example community is in Georgia and has a population of 16,000, use service standards for Southern communities with population of 10,000 to 24,999. Multiply these standards (2.01 police per 1000 population) by anticipated project population of 7,550 residents. The development therefore generates a need for approximately 15 (7.550 × 2.01 = 15.8) police (see Exhibit 4, column 4 for calculation for other services).
3	Calculate average operating expenses per employee by service category by dividing total operating expenses per service category by the total number of employees in that function.	The Georgia community expends $480,795 for its 35 member police force. Operating costs per employee are therefore $13,737 ($\frac{480{,}795}{35}$).
4	Project total annual operating costs by multiplying average operating expenses per worker by the number of employees attributable to growth.	The development generates $208,528 (15.18 × $13,737) in police operating costs (see Exhibit 4, column 6 for calculations for other services).
5	Project total annual capital costs attributable to growth by multiplying capital-to-operating expenditure ratios by total annual operating cost.	Capital-to-operating expenditure ratios are selected in the same manner as service standards. Capital costs are projected by multiplying predicted operating outlays by capital-to-operating expenditure ratios. The development generates $11,261 in police capital costs (see Exhibit 4, column 8 for calculations for other services).

Government Function	Total Annual Operating Costs by Function	Capital-to-Operating Ratios for Population Size Group and Region	Total Annual Capital Costs by Function
Police	$208,528	.054	$11,261

STEP NUMBER	ANALYSIS/ACTIONS	EXAMPLE CALCULATION
6	Project total annual costs by adding total annual operating expenses to total annual capital expenses.	The 2,000 unit single-family development generates $208,528 in police operating expenditures and $11,261 in police capital costs for a total of $219,789 in police costs (see Exhibit 4, column 9 for calculations for other services).

EXHIBIT 4

EXAMPLE FISCAL IMPACT COST PROJECTION USING THE SERVICE STANDARD METHOD

USING THE SERVICE STANDARD METHOD TO PROJECT THE FISCAL IMPACT OF LAND USE ALTERNATIVES: LAND USE ALTERNATIVE 1

Step 1 Anticipated Population and Public School-Age Children (1)	Step 1 Government Functions (2)	Step 2 Manpower Ratios for Population Size Group and Region (3)	Step 2 Estimated Number of Future Employees[1] (4)	Step 3 Operating Expenses Per Future Employee (5)	Step 4 Total Annual Operating Costs by Function[2] (6)	Step 5 Capital-to Operating Ratios for Population Size Group and Region (7)	Step 5 Total Annual Capital Costs by Function[3] (8)	Step 6 Total Annual Public Costs (Operating + Capital) by Function[4] (9)
LAND USE ALTERNATIVE 1 7,550 Population 1,989 Public School-Age Children								
	MUNICIPAL FUNCTIONS							
	GENERAL GOVERNMENT							
	Finance Administration	.46	3.47	$14,333	$ 49,736	.000	—	$ 49,736
	General Control	.58	4.38	9,736	42,644	.000	—	42,644
	PUBLIC SAFETY							
	Police	2.01	15.18	13,737	208,528	.054	$ 11,261	219,789
	Fire	1.24	9.36	14,205	132,959	.026	3,457	136,416
	PUBLIC WORKS							
	Highways	1.12	8.46	12,942	109,489	.199	21,788	131,277
	Sewerage	.53	4.00	13,267	53,068	.147	7,801	60,869
	Sanitation	1.47	11.10	11,580	128,538	.078	10,026	138,564
	Water Supply	.94	7.10	12,904	91,618	.226	20,706	112,324
	RECREATION & CULTURE							
	Parks and Recreation	.58	4.38	8,883	38,908	.097	3,774	42,682
	Libraries	.12	.91	9,282	8,447	.000	—	8,447
	Total Municipal				863,935		78,813	942,748
	SCHOOL DISTRICT							
	Primary/Secondary Schools	78	155.14	11,800	1,830,652	.073	133,638	1,964,290
	Total School District				1,830,652		133,638	1,964,290
	TOTAL MUNICIPAL AND SCHOOL DISTRICT				2,694,587		212,451	2,907,038

Notes: 1 Anticipated population (7,550) and (1,989) public school-age children (expressed in 000s as 7,550 and 1,989, respectively) multiplied by service ratios shown in column 3.
2 Column 4 multiplied by column 5.
3 Column 6 multiplied by column 7.
4 Column 6 plus column 8.

Source: U.S. Census of Governments, 1972.

EXHIBIT 5

SERVICE STANDARDS FOR FULL TIME PUBLIC EMPLOYMENT (SOUTHERN REGION)

FULL-TIME EMPLOYEES PER 1,000 POPULATION AND PUPILS FOR MUNICIPAL AND SCHOOL DISTRICT SERVICES, BY MUNICIPAL/SCHOOL DISTRICT SIZE AND REGION OF THE UNITED STATES[1] (SOUTHERN REGION[2])

Municipal Population Size (Number of Residents)	Less Than 2,500 (Use for Municipal[3] Functions)	2,500 to 4,999	5,000 to 9,999	10,000 to 24,999	25,000 to 49,999	50,000 to 99,999	100,000 to 199,999	200,000 to 299,999	300,000 to 499,999	500,000 to 999,999	1,000,000 And Over
MUNICIPAL FUNCTIONS											
GENERAL GOVERNMENT											
Finance Administration	0.33	0.46	0.43	0.46	0.52	0.57	0.70	0.44	0.38	0.57	0.22
General Control	0.67	0.81	0.77	0.58	0.53	0.55	0.49	0.48	0.51	1.04	0.25
PUBLIC SAFETY											
Police	1.54	1.96	2.14	2.01	2.01	2.17	2.32	2.28	2.29	3.83	2.03
Fire	0.41	0.62	0.91	1.24	1.64	1.75	1.76	1.72	1.76	1.91	1.69
PUBLIC WORKS											
Highways	0.80	1.09	1.25	1.12	1.00	0.95	0.92	0.97	0.78	0.87	0.53
Sewerage	—	0.42	0.42	0.53	0.53	0.52	0.41	0.70	0.56	0.56	0.35
Sanitation	0.02	1.38	1.51	1.47	1.44	1.44	1.55	1.35	1.25	1.49	0.63
Water Supply	0.01	0.78	0.83	0.94	0.99	0.95	0.90	0.72	1.02	1.06	0.78
RECREATION AND CULTURE											
Parks and Recreation	—	0.16	0.37	0.58	0.82	1.00	0.96	1.29	1.12	1.22	0.56
Libraries	—	0.05	0.08	0.12	0.17	0.20	0.26	1.33	0.31	0.51	0.27

SCHOOL DISTRICT FUNCTION	School District Enrollment (Number of Students) *(Use for Education[4])*		
	Less than 1,200	1,200-2,999	3,000 and over
Primary and Secondary Schools	77	78	78

Notes:

1 These figures are read as follows: In a municipality whose population falls between 2,500 and 4,999 there are, on the average, 1.96 full-time employees in the police department per 1,000 population. In a school district whose enrollment (pupils) falls between 1,200 and 2,999 there are, on the average, 78 full-time employees in primary, secondary and special education services per 1,000 pupils.

2 Includes Alabama, Arkansas, Delaware, Florida, Georgia, Kentucky, Louisiana, Maryland, Mississippi, North Carolina, Oklahoma, South Carolina, Tennessee, Texas, Virginia, Washington, D.C., West Virginia.

3 Use the multipliers above the dotted line for municipal functions.

4 Use the multipliers below the dotted line for school district functions.

Source: U.S. Census of Government, 1972.

Advantages/Disadvantages

Advantages

Richness of Detail The Service Standard Method is second only to the Case Study Method in the amount of detail it provides. The Service Standard technique not only predicts the financial consequences of population change but also traces specific growth-induced responses for each public service category.

Simplicity/Low Cost The Service Standard technique is straightforward and inexpensive to use.

Disadvantages

To the extent that actual local performance differs from the average (due to variance in local wealth, excess or deficient service capacity situations, labor rules or traditions, public service emphases) the Service Standard projection will either overestimate or underestimate true local expenditures.

Practitioner's Notes

(1) Point out to users the versatility of U.S. Census data as opposed to previously used trade union or employment association standards, etc.
(2) Method may be used when only rough gauges of future resident and school populations are available.
(3) Capital-to-operating ratios replace myriad of standards for individual capital facilities.
(4) Standards are available for "common categories of municipal expenditure" as defined by Census of Governments. For service categories other than these, other standards must be used.
(5) Standards are relatively stable over time. Multipliers appear to peak in 1968 and remain slightly lower and level from this period on.
(6) Local "standards", derived from the specific service experience of the city being analyzed may be used in place of national standards.

COMPARABLE CITY METHOD

Background

The Comparable City Method is used to project marginal fiscal impact. It relies on expenditure multipliers that vary by size and growth rate of community or school district. The multipliers, presented in chart form, represent a proportional relationship of the average expenditures of cities of various size and growth rates to the average expenditures of cities of the most common population size and growth rate. As a community grows or declines at a certain pace, and in so doing changes population categories, its expenditure pattern is characterized by a different multiplier. The ratio of the new multiplier to the old multiplier is multiplied by existing per capita expenditures to determine the new local municipal and school district costs resulting from change. The expenditure multipliers have been derived from data compiled by the U.S. Census of Governments and are available in sixteen increments for community size and growth rate. Briefly, the method projects increases or decreases in future gross expenditures for the five basic municipal services (general government, public safety, public works, health and welfare, recreation and culture) by comparing the products of a community's expenditure ratios, per capita costs, and service populations before and after a projected growth increment.

To illustrate, a municipality with a population of 49,000 and a historical annual growth rate of 0.4 percent rezones land to accommodate a large planned development. This development will house 10,000 residents and be built over a five-year period. The community will thus grow to a level of 59,000 with a 4 percent annual growth rate over the period of its construction (10,000/49,000 = .20/5yrs. = .04/yr.). Its pregrowth general government operating expenditure ratio is .97 (from Exhibit 7—communities of 25,001 to 50,000 population and 0 to .5 percent annual growth rate); its postgrowth operating expenditure ratio is 1.21 (communities of 50,000 to 100,000 population and over 2 percent annual growth rate). Assuming that before development the community exhibited a $20 per capita general government operating expenditure, then if this community behaves in a fashion similar to other communities of this post-growth population size and growth rate, it may anticipate that future expenditures for general government purposes will be $25 per person ($20 x 1.21/.97 = $25).

Multiplying this figure by the present plus the increment in service population, the community will experience (based on historic trends of the similar communities) $1,475,000 in total general government operating expenditures (59,000 x $25). Since prior to development it spent $980,000 annually for this service (49,000 x $20), the general government operating expense engendered by the large planned development, and thus assignable to this growth, is $495,000 annually ($1,475,000 minus $980,000). This projection procedure for operating and capital expenditures is repeated for each of the basic municipal and school district functions (i.e., public safety, public works, health/welfare, recreation/culture) to determine total costs assignable to future growth.

Assumptions

A basic assumption of the Comparable City Method is that public service expenditures vary significantly according to a community's size and growth rate.

A second assumption is that the direction of growth (positive or negative) also affects local service expenditures.

Data Requirements

The most important data to implement the Comparable City Method are the expenditure multipliers for municipal and school district services, by community size and growth rate. These are available in the *Guidebook*.

Procedures and Example Calculations

See pp. 25-27

COMPARABLE CITY FISCAL IMPACT ANALYSIS METHOD:
SUMMARY OF COST PROJECTION PROCEDURES

STEP NUMBER	ANALYSIS/ACTIONS	EXAMPLE CALCULATION (A 2,000 UNIT SINGLE-FAMILY DEVELOPMENT IS PROPOSED IN A CALIFORNIA COMMUNITY OF 16,000. ILLUSTRATIVE CALCULATIONS ARE FOR PUBLIC SAFETY COSTS ONLY. SEE EXHIBIT 6 FOR CALCULATIONS FOR ALL PUBLIC SERVICES.)
1	Using blended multipliers for household size and school-age children, determine the magnitude and rate of population/student growth.	As example community is in California, use demographic multipliers for Western region, Pacific subregion. These multipliers indicate a total development generated population of 7,652 residents and 2,284 public school-age children.
2	Using the population projected in step 1, select appropriate expenditure multipliers and determine the rate of change in these multipliers.	As example community has an annual growth rate of 1.7% and has a population of 16,000, use current expenditure multipliers for communities of 10,000-25,000 population and an annual growth rate of 1.5 to 2.0 percent. As development will increase the community's population to 23,652 (16,000 + 7,652) and the community's annual growth rate to over 2 percent, use future expenditure multipliers for communities of 10,000-25,000 population and an annual growth rate of over 2 percent. The future-to-current expenditure multiplier ratio is determined by dividing the future expenditure multipliers by the current expenditure multipliers. For public safety service the following multipliers are therefore used (see Exhibit 6, columns 3 to 5 for multipliers for other services):

Current expenditure Multipliers		Future Expenditure Multipliers		Future-Current Expenditure Multiplier Ratio	
Operating	Capital	Operating	Capital	Operating	Capital
0.82	0.81	0.82	1.00	1.00	1.23

STEP NUMBER	ANALYSIS/ACTIONS	EXAMPLE CALCULATION
3	Divide total operating and capital outlays for each service category by the existing local population to calculate current average operating and capital expenditures per capita.	The California community expends $38.52 in public safety per capita operating costs and $5.15 in public safety per capita capital costs.
4	Project future per capita cost by service category by multiplying the per capita expenditures determined in step 3 by the multiplier rate-of-change ratios calculated in step 2.	Current per capita costs are multiplied by the future-to-current expenditure multiplier ratios to determine future per capita costs. For public safety the following numbers are used (see Exhibit, column 7 for other public service calculations):

Future-current Expenditure Multiplier Ratio		X	Current Annual Per Capita Expenditure		=	Future Annual Expenditure Per Capita	
Operating	Capital		Operating	Capital		Operating	Capital
1.00	1.23		$38.52	$5.15		$38.52	$6.33

COMPARABLE CITY FISCAL IMPACT ANALYSIS METHOD (Continued)

5   Determine future net annual costs by multiplying the future expenditures per person and per pupil by the community's future population and then subtracting the costs that would be incurred even if there were no growth.

Future annual costs equal the future per capita expenditures multiplied by the future total population. The net cost attributed to an incoming development equals the difference between what costs will be (future annual costs) and what they are today (current annual costs). The 2,000 unit single-family development therefore generates $362,072 in public safety costs:

Future Annual Expenditure Per Capita		Future Municipal Population	Future Total Annual Expenditures		Current Annual Expenditures		Net Annual Expenditures		
Operating	Capital		Operating	Capital	Operating	Capital	Operating	Capital	TOTAL
$38.52	$6.33	23,652	$911,075	$149,717	$616,320	$82,400	$294,755	$67,317	$362,072

Advantages/Disadvantages

Advantages

Time and Cost The Comparable City Method is relatively inexpensive to effect. Time requirements to employ this method are about the same as the Service Standard Method.

Disadvantages

Validity of the Expenditure Multipliers The Comparable City Method assumes that local operating and capital expenditures attributable to growth will, in the long run, emulate the expense patterns of communities of comparable size and growth rate. If local costs differ from the patterns indicated by the expenditure multipliers of comparable cities, average expenditure multipliers used to predict local response to population change, may tend to either under or overestimate the true reaction.

Practitioner's Notes

(1) A precondition for employment of this method is future population levels and/or growth rates significantly different from what is currently being experienced.
(2) An assumption is that the service profile of the size-average of communities to which you will grow, via a different than current growth rate, is the best indication of future expected service loads.
(3) Make sure that information is selected from the correct growth *direction* cell, i.e. positive or negative. Often the user has growth magnitude correct but forgets directions of growth and selects from the wrong cell.
(4) This is a severe view of cost impact as new servicing costs levels are assigned to the *entire* population.

EXHIBIT 6

EXAMPLE FISCAL IMPACT COST PROJECTION USING THE COMPARABLE CITY METHOD

USING THE COMPARABLE CITY METHOD TO EVALUATE THE FISCAL IMPACT OF LAND USE ALTERNATIVES

Step 1: Anticipated Increments of Population and School-age Children (1)	Governmental Functions (2)	Step 2: Current Expenditure Multipliers Op (3)	Cap (3)	Step 2: Future Expenditure Multipliers Op (4)	Cap (4)	Step 2: Future-Current Expenditure Multiplier Ratio Op (5)	Cap (5)	Step 3: Current-Annual Expenditure per Person/Pupil Op (6)	Cap (6)	Step 4: Future-Annual Expenditure per Person/Pupil Op (7)	Cap (7)	Step 5: Future Total Annual Expenditures Op (8)	Cap (8)	Step 5: Current Total Annual Expenditures Op (9)	Cap (9)	Step 5: Net Annual Cost by Function Op (10)	Cap (10)	Total Operating and Capital Costs
LAND USE ALTERNATIVE 1 **MUNICIPAL**																		
2000 single-family homes (average market value—$50,000)	General government	0.96	0.21	0.86	0.49	0.90	2.33	15.54	1.93	13.99	4.50	$ 330,891	$ 106,434	$ 248,640	$ 30,880	$ 82,251	$ 75,554	$ 157,805
	Public safety	0.82	0.81	0.82	0.81	1.00	1.00	38.52	5.15	38.52	6.33	911,075	149,717	616,320	82,400	294,755	67,317	362,072
	Public works	1.19	0.42	1.05	0.75	0.88	1.79	48.80	13.49	42.94	24.15	1,015,617	571,196	780,800	215,840	234,817	355,356	590,173
	Health and welfare	0.58	0.67	0.58	0.83	1.00	1.24	4.10	0.65	4.10	0.81	96,973	19,158	65,600	10,400	31,373	8,758	40,131
	Recreation and culture	0.77	0.36	0.64	0.56	0.83	1.56	5.50	0.81	4.57	1.26	108,090	29,802	88,000	12,960	20,090	16,842	36,932
	TOTAL MUNICIPAL											$2,462,646	$ 876,307	$1,799,360	$352,480	$ 663,286	$ 523,827	$1,187,113
7,652 Population 2,259 School-age children	*SCHOOL DISTRICT* Primary/secondary schools	1.03	1.19	1.03	1.19	1.00	1.00	$1,217.00	$80.00	$1,217.00	$80.00	$9,442,720	$620,720	$6,693,500	$440,000	$2,749,203	$ 180,720	$2,929,923
	TOTAL MUNICIPAL AND SCHOOL DISTRICT																	
LAND USE ALTERNATIVE 2 **MUNICIPAL**																		
Mixed-use development (2500 townhouses 1500 single-family homes, 1,000 condominiums) (average market value—$35,000)	General government	0.96	0.21	1.00	1.00	1.04	4.76	15.54	1.93	16.16	9.19	$ 513,339	$ 291,930	$ 248,640	$ 30,880	$ 264,699	$ 261,050	$ 525,749
	Public safety	0.82	0.81	1.00	1.00	1.22	1.23	38.52	5.15	46.99	6.33	1,492,684	201,079	616,320	82,400	876,364	118,679	995,043
	Public works	1.19	0.42	1.00	1.00	0.84	2.38	48.80	13.49	40.99	32.11	1,302,088	1,020,006	780,800	215,840	521,288	804,166	1,325,454
	Health and welfare	0.58	0.67	1.00	1.00	1.72	1.49	4.10	0.65	7.05	0.97	223,950	30,813	65,600	10,400	158,350	20,413	178,763
	Recreation and culture	0.77	0.36	1.00	1.00	1.30	2.78	5.50	0.81	7.15	2.25	227,127	71,474	88,000	12,960	139,127	58,514	197,641
	TOTAL MUNICIPAL											$3,759,188	$1,615,302	$1,799,360	$352,480	$1,959,828	$1,262,822	$3,222,650
15,652 Population 3,968 School-age children	*SCHOOL DISTRICT* Primary/secondary schools	1.03	1.19	1.03	1.19	1.00	1.00	$1,217.00	$80.00	$1,217.00	$80.00	$11,522,556	$757,400	$6,693,500	$440,000	$4,829,056	$ 317,400	$5,146,496
	TOTAL MUNICIPAL AND SCHOOL DISTRICT																	$8,369,146
LAND USE ALTERNATIVE 3 **MUNICIPAL**																		
7000 garden apartments (average rental $250/Mo.)	General government	0.96	0.27	1.00	1.00	1.04	4.76	16.00	1.93	16.16	9.19	$ 501,655	$ 285,285	$ 248,640	$ 30,880	$ 253,015	$ 254,405	$ 507,420
	Public safety	0.82	0.81	1.00	1.00	1.22	1.23	38.52	5.15	46.99	6.33	1,458,711	196,502	616,320	82,400	842,391	114,102	956,493
	Public works	1.19	0.42	1.00	1.00	0.84	2.38	48.80	13.49	40.99	32.11	1,272,453	996,791	780,800	215,840	491,653	780,951	1,272,604
	Health and welfare	0.58	0.67	1.00	1.00	1.72	1.49	4.10	0.65	7.05	0.97	218,853	30,112	65,600	10,400	153,253	19,712	172,965
	Recreation and culture	0.77	0.36	1.00	1.00	1.30	2.78	5.50	0.81	7.15	2.25	221,957	69,847	88,000	12,960	133,957	56,887	190,844
	TOTAL MUNICIPAL											$3,673,629	$1,578,537	$1,799,360	$352,480	$1,874,269	$1,226,057	$3,100,326
15,043 Population 1,827 School-age children	*SCHOOL DISTRICT* Primary/secondary schools	1.03	1.19	1.03	1.19	1.00	1.00	$1,217.00	$80.00	$1,217.00	$80.00	$8,916,959	$586,160	$6,693,500	$440,000	$2,223,459	$ 146,160	$2,369,619
	TOTAL MUNICIPAL AND SCHOOL DISTRICT																	$5,469,945

Notes: Column (5) equals column (4) divided by column (3).
Column (7) equals column (6) multiplied by column (5).
Column (8) equals column (7) multiplied by total *future* population.
Column (9) equals column (6) multiplied by total *current* population.
Column (10) equals column (8) minus column (9).

EXHIBIT 7

OPERATING EXPENDITURE MULTIPLIERS BY POPULATION SIZE AND GROWTH RATE

MUNICIPAL AND SCHOOL DISTRICT MEDIAN OPERATING EXPENDITURE MULTIPLIERS BY POPULATION SIZE AND GROWTH RATE

Municipal Population (Number of Residents) (Use for Municipal Functions)	(1) 1,000- 10,000	(2) 10,001- 25,000	(3) 25,001- 50,000	(4) 50,001- 100,000	(5) 100,001- 500,000	(6) 500,001- 1,000,000	(7) Over 1,000,000
1.5% to 2.0% increase							
General Government	0.82	0.96	1.22	1.01	1.37	N/A*	N/A
Public Safety	0.61	0.82	1.21	1.41	1.28	N/A	N/A
Public Works	1.14	1.19	1.14	1.22	1.28	N/A	N/A
Health/Welfare	0.04	0.58	0.77	1.63	3.16	N/A	N/A
Recreation/Culture	0.48	0.77	0.95	1.11	1.51	N/A	N/A
Education	1.02	0.99	1.00	1.03	1.08	1.04	1.07
over 2.0% increase							
General Government	0.81	0.86	1.00	1.21	1.19	1.30	N/A
Public Safety	0.62	0.82	1.00	1.24	1.39	1.47	N/A
Public Works	1.05	1.05	1.00	0.98	1.04	1.06	N/A
Health/Welfare	0.04	0.58	1.00	0.20	0.54	2.98	N/A
Recreation/Culture	0.44	0.64	1.00	1.37	1.50	1.76	N/A
Education	1.02	0.99	1.00	1.03	1.08	1.04	1.07
0% to 0.5% decrease							
General Government	0.69	0.97	1.23	1.59	1.47	2.35	N/A
Public Safety	0.58	0.94	1.09	1.40	1.61	3.38	N/A
Public Works	1.10	1.21	1.26	1.21	1.20	1.51	N/A
Health/Welfare	0.04	0.32	0.86	1.48	3.97	4.44	N/A
Recreation/Culture	0.40	0.89	1.02	1.13	1.51	3.11	N/A
Education	1.02	0.99	1.00	1.03	1.08	1.04	1.07
School District Enrollment (Number of Students) (Use for Education)	Less than 1,200	1,200- 2,499	2,500- 4,999	5,000- 9,999	10,000- 24,999	25,000- 99,999	100,000- And Over

* Data not available.

Source: U.S. Census of Governments, 1972. These figures are to be read as follows: In a municipality whose size falls between 10,001 and 25,000 and has a growth rate between 1.5% and 2.0%, the appropriate median general government operating expenditure multiplier is 0.96. In a school district whose enrollment (pupils) falls at less than 1,200, the appropriate median operating expenditure multiplier is 1.02.

PROPORTIONAL VALUATION METHOD

Background

The Proportional Valuation Method is an average costing approach used to project the impact of *nonresidential (industrial and commercial)* development on local costs and revenues. Because data on real property value are almost universally maintained, analysts have regularly used this method, like the Case Study, to assess the municipal fiscal implications of commercial and industrial growth.

The Proportional Valuation Method employs a two-step process to assign a share of municipal costs to a new commercial or industrial establishment. First, a share of total municipal costs is given to all local nonresidential uses. Second, a portion of these nonresidential costs is allocated to the incoming nonresidential facility. The method assumes that relative real property values represent shares of municipal costs. Experience has shown, however, that while the direction of this cost assignment procedure is relatively accurate, as the value of nonresidential property significantly differs from the average value of existing local property, the direct proportional assignment of costs tends either to overstate or understate the magnitude of assignable costs. Thus, the analyst must use refinement coefficients to compensate for this over- or under-statement of costs, and to modify the direct proportional relationship in the allocation of municipal costs.

To illustrate, a local shopping center, valued at $5,000,000, is proposed for a Texas community whose total property valuation is $100,000,000 ($80,000,000 residential, farm, and vacant land, and $20,000,000 for commercial and industrial property). Annual municipal operating expenditures, including statutory and capital debt service costs, are $3,500,000.

The analyst using the Proportional Valuation Method first assigns a share of the $3,500,000 annual municipal operating expenditures to all local nonresidential uses. To do so, he multiplies all municipal costs by the product of local nonresidential real property valuation to total local real property valuation (in this example $20,000,000/$100,000,000 or 0.20) and a refinement coefficient (1.38). The resulting share is $966,000. He next assigns a share of these costs to the incoming nonresidential facility by multiplying total nonresidential costs by the product of the real property valuation of the new facility to total local nonresidential valuation ($5,000,000/$20,000,000 or 0.25) and a refinement coefficient (0.18). The result is $43,470. Costs are then partitioned into the six categories of municipal service, using percentage distributions which have been derived from case studies, of other industrial and commercial fiscal impact.

Assumptions

A basic assumption of the Proportional Valuation Method is that municipal costs increase with the intensity of land use, and change in real property value is a reasonable substitute for change in intensity of use. Further, as nonresidential real property value departs significantly from the average local real property value, the direct proportional relationship must be refined to avoid either overstating (where incremental or average nonresidential real property value significantly exceeds average local property values) or understating costs (where incremental or average nonresidential real property value is significantly less than average local property value).

Data Requirements

The Proportional Valuation Method requires a limited amount of data; most of it is readily available. The most important segment of information is the equalized real property value—for the new nonresidential facility, for all nonresidential real property, and for all local real property. Refinement coefficients, to scale the costs to all nonresidential property and to the new nonresidential facility, are found in the *Guidebook*.

Procedures and Example Calculations

See pp. 31-32

Advantages/Disadvantages

Advantages

Time and Cost The Proportional Valuation Method may be completed quickly and inexpensively. Approximately thirty hours are required to implement this approach. This time factor, while comparable to the Employee Anticipation Method, is far less than the time required to complete a Case Study.

Disadvantages

Validity of the Refinement Coefficients Two sets of refinement coefficients are employed to improve the accuracy of the Proportional Valuation Method. They are derived from retrospective analyses which compared the actual expenditures generated by nonresidential facilities to those projected using a simple proportional valuation strategy. The refinement coefficients are initial approximations which must be significantly expanded in the future.

Practitioner's Notes

(1) The Proportional Valuation Method should *not* be used for residential analyses— more accurate methods are available for residential fiscal impact.
(2) Refinement coefficients are necessary because this technique frequently understates the impact of low value facilities and overstates the impact of high value facilities.
(3) The method provides only rough estimates: resources permitting, back-up should be undertaken with a Case Study.
(4) Refinement coefficients can be replaced with a weighted average of department heads' estimates of the proportion of services allocated to nonresidential versus residential uses.

PROPORTIONAL VALUATION FISCAL IMPACT METHOD: SUMMARY OF COST PROJECTION PROCEDURES

STEP NUMBER	ANALYSIS/ACTIONS	EXAMPLE CALCULATION (A 100,000 ft.² SHOPPING CENTER IS PROPOSED IN A TEXAS COMMUNITY. SEE EXHIBIT 8.)
1	Obtain basic data including municipal expenditures, real property valuation, and land parcel characteristics of the locality where the cost revenue analysis is being conducted.	The Texas community has the following expenditures/property values: Total municipal expenditures: $2,692,051 Total real property value: $134,734,889 Nonresidential real property value: $41,841,111 Incoming facility nonresidential property value: $4,000,000
2	Assign a share of existing municipal expenditures to existing total nonresidential uses by using proportional valuation and refinement coefficients applied toward total local municipal expenditures.	The proportion of nonresidential value to total local property value is .31 ($41,841,111). The refinement coefficient is derived by comparing the ($134,734,880) average value of nonresidential parcels to the average value of all parcels (see Exhibit 8). Total nonresidential induced municipal expenditures are therefore:
		Total Existing Municipal Expenditures Attributable to Nonresidential Uses = Total Local Municipal Expenditures × Proportion of Nonresidential Value to Total Local Real Property Value × Refinement Coefficient
		$1,084,897 = $2,692,051 × (.31) × (1.30)
3	Project future total annual nonresidential costs induced by nonresidential facility being studied by using proportional valuation and refinement coefficients applied toward total local municipal expenditures induced by growth.	The proportion of incoming facility to total local nonresidential property value is .096 ($4,000,000). The refinement coefficient is derived by comparing the ($41,841,111) value of the new nonresidential facility to the average value of local nonresidential parcels (see Exhibit 8). The municipal costs generated by the incoming facility are therefore:
		Municipal Costs Allocated to the Nonresidential Facility = Total Existing Municipal Expenditures Attributable to Nonresidential Uses × Proportion of Facility to Total Local Nonresidential Real Property Value × Refinement Coefficient
		$15,623 = $1,084,897 × (.096) × (.15)
4	Assign total annual nonresidential facility costs to service categories (general government, public safety, public works, etc.).	Case studies reveal that commercial facilities have the largest impact on public safety and public works services. Other services are only minimally affected. These case studies suggest the following disaggregation of total projected expenditures:

	Distribution of Total Costs	
Municipal Service Category	Percentage	Dollars
General Government	6	$ 937
Public Safety	75	11,717
Public Works	15	2,343
Health and Welfare	2	313
Recreation and Culture	2	313
TOTAL	100	$15,623

EXHIBIT 8

EXAMPLE FISCAL IMPACT COST PROJECTION USING
THE PROPORTIONAL VALUATION METHOD

USING THE PROPORTIONAL VALUATION METHOD TO PROJECT THE FISCAL IMPACT
OF A PROPOSED NONRESIDENTIAL DEVELOPMENT

LOCAL NONRESIDENTIAL USE COST PROJECTION   (Step 2)

Total Existing Municipal Expenditures Attributable to Nonresidential Uses		*Total Municipal Expenditures*	X	*Proportion of Nonresidential Value to Total Local Real Property Value*[1]	X	*Refinement Coefficient*[2]
	=					
		$2,692,051	X	($ 41,841,111) / 134,734,889)	X	1.30)
$1,084,897		$2,692,051	X	(.31	X	1.30)

INCOMING NONRESIDENTIAL USE COST PROJECTION   (Step 3)

Municipal Costs Allocated to the Incoming Nonresidential Facility		*Total Existing Municipal Expenditures Attributable to Nonresidential Uses*	X	*Proportion of Facility to Total Local Nonresidential Real Property Value*[3]	X	*Refinement Coefficient*[4]
	=					
		$1,084,897	X	($ 4,000,000 / 41,841,111	X	.15)
$ 15,623		$1,084,897	X	(.096	X	.15)

INCOMING NONRESIDENTIAL USE COST DISTRIBUTION   (Step 4)

	Distribution of Total Costs	
	Percentage[5]	Dollars
Municipal Service Category*		
General Government	6	$ 937
Public Safety	75	11,717
Public Works	15	2,343
Health and Welfare	2	313
Recreation and Culture	2	313
TOTAL	100	$15,623

* Includes statutory and capital debt service costs

1 Simple Proportional Valuation = $\dfrac{\text{Existing Total Local Nonresidential Real Property Value}}{\text{Total Local Real Property Value}}$

2 The value multiplier for the refinement coefficient is determined by comparing the average value of nonresidential parcels to the average value of all parcels.

3 Simple Proportional Valuation = $\dfrac{\text{Subject Nonresidential Real Property Value}}{\text{Existing Total Nonresidential Real Property Value}}$

4 The value multiplier for the refinement coefficient is determined by comparing the value of the new nonresidential facility to the average value of local nonresidential parcels.

5 Percentage distribution for commercial nonresidential uses.

EXHIBIT 9

REFINEMENT COEFFICIENTS FOR THE PROPORTIONAL VALUATION FISCAL IMPACT METHOD

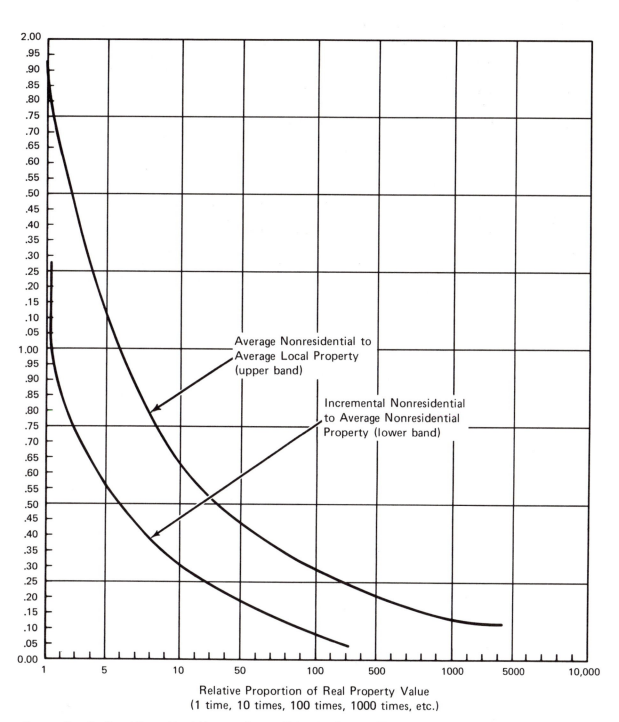

Relative Proportion of Real Property Value
(1 time, 10 times, 100 times, 1000 times, etc.)

Source: Case Studies of Nonresidential Impact—Rutgers University, Spring, 1977.

EMPLOYMENT ANTICIPATION METHOD

Background

The Employment Anticipation Method is a recently developed marginal costing technique for projecting the impact of *nonresidential (industrial and commercial)* growth on local municipal costs and revenues. The method relies on relationships between local commercial and industrial employment levels and per capita municipal costs. It predicts a change in municipal costs based on an anticipated change in local commercial or industrial employment levels and per capita municipal costs. Coefficients for the five categories of municipal service (general government, public safety, public works, health/welfare, recreation/culture) and for statutory/unclassified expenses and debt service have been developed using multivariate regression analysis to predict the change in municipal expenditures related to local employment variation. The coefficients may be read as "a change of one commercial or industrial employee will produce an increase in per capita local public service expenditures of X percent."

To illustrate, assume that a new industrial plant with 1,000 employees will be built in a growing community whose current population is 16,000 and whose current per capita public safety cost is $50.00. The cost for this service generated by the new facility is calculated by first multiplying the percentage increase per employee for public safety (0.00162) by the number of employees (1,000), which yields an increase in the per capita costs of public safety of 1.62 percent. Per capita outlays will therefore rise by $.81 ($50.00 X 0.0162 = $.81); from $50.00 to $50.81. Multiplying the resident population by the increase in costs ($16,000 X $.81) yields the total increase in operating costs ($12,960) for public safety assignable to the new industrial plant. This procedure is repeated for each of the remaining categories of municipal service and for aggregate statutory and capital (debt service) expenditures to determine total annual municipal costs related to growth. Revenues are tabulated in the same way as for the other methods and compared with costs to determine net fiscal impact.

Assumptions

The Employment Anticipation Method is based on three assumptions: (1) the level of local commercial or industrial employment directly affects the magnitude of local municipal expenditures; (2) the relationship viewed is the impact of commercial or industrial employment on municipal expenditures within a multivariate context, controlling for the confounding effects of other social, political, and economic factors; (3) the impact of additional employment will vary for communities of differing population size and direction of growth.

Data Requirements

Data required for the Employment Anticipation Method consists of four elements: (1) existing per capita expenditures by service category, (2) coefficients of per capita percent change per employee, (3) projections of future employees by nonresidential type; and (4) current municipal population estimates.

Procedures and Example Calculations

See pp. 36-37

Advantages and Disadvantages

Advantages

Operational Utility An obvious advantage of the Employment Anticipation Method is that it expresses future municipal costs as a function of expected employees—the direct local product of nonresidential growth.

Simplicity/Cost The Employment Anticipation Method is inexpensive to use. It is similar in scope to the Proportional Valuation Method.

Disadvantages

This method relies on coefficients to express changes in per capita municipal expenditures for categories of cities defined by population size and direction of growth. In so doing, a single multiplier is used for all cities within a particular population group. Since cities may vary by populations of close to 50,000 for the larger groups, the same nonresidential facility in a city of 149,000 may be shown to be significantly more costly than one in a city of 100,000. Obviously this is not the case. It is the grouping technique that limits the result.

Practitioner's Notes

(1) Emphasize that changes in a city's employment are viewed simultaneously with other changes taking place in city structure (i.e., income, wealth, tax base, etc.). The specific effect of employment change on municipal expenditures is then segregated from other internal socioeconomic changes and specified as to magnitude.
(2) The Employment Anticipation Method does not provide coefficients for cities over 150,000. This is due to the data base that was used (New Jersey municipalities), which contained only a few cities in excess of 150,000 and were subsequently eliminated for insufficiency of sample. If nonresidential development is contemplated for cities over 150,000, the Case Study Method should be used.
(3) High impact costs in statutory/unclassified and debt service costs reflect liberal retirement benefits and capital facility expansions of the early 1970s.

EMPLOYMENT ANTICIPATION FISCAL IMPACT METHOD: SUMMARY OF COST PROJECTION PROCEDURES

EXAMPLE CALCULATION (A 100,000 ft² INDUSTRIAL BUILDING IS PROPOSED IN A COMMUNITY OF 16,000. ILLUSTRATIVE CALCULATIONS ARE FOR PUBLIC SAFETY COSTS ONLY. SEE EXHIBIT 10 FOR CALCULATIONS FOR ALL PUBLIC SERVICES.)

STEP NUMBER	ANALYSIS/ACTIONS	EXAMPLE CALCULATION
1	Using information from the published local budget and the most recent population estimate, determine per capita municipal expenditures by service category.	This example community has a $726,400 annual expenditure for public safety. Per capita public safety costs are therefore $45.40 ($726,400 ÷ 16,000).
2	Obtain anticipated employment for the new commercial or industrial facility from developer estimates or by multiplying the square footage of the new facility by the average number of employees per square foot for a comparable facility.	As comparable commercial facilities employ one worker per 300 ft², the proposed 100,000 ft² commercial structure will employ 333 workers $\left(333 = \dfrac{100,000}{300}\right)$.
3	Using the known direction of growth over the previous decade and current population size, choose the applicable percentage increase per employee, by service category, for municipal service costs.	As example community is: (1) growing in population; (2) currently contains 16,000 residents; and (3) incoming commercial use is an industrial facility, use industrial employment anticipation multipliers for growing communities of 10,000 to 24,999 population (see Exhibit 11). The public safety multiplier for the example community is 0.0000162 (see Exhibit 10, column 4 for multipliers for other services).
4	Multiply the new employment increment by the percentage increase in costs per employee to determine total percentage increase for each service.	*Percentage increase in costs per public safety employee* = *Public safety multiplier* × *Expected number of employees* .005395 = .0000162 × 333 (See Exhibit 10, column 6 for calculations for other public services.)
5	Multiply the percentage increase in per capita expenditures by service category by the existing per capita expenditures in that service category to determine the dollar increase per capita for each service.	*Dollar increase in per capita public safety costs* = *Public safety per capita cost* × *Percentage change in costs per public safety employee* $0.244933 = $45.40 × .005395 (See Exhibit 10, column 8 for calculations for other public services.)
6	Multiply the increase in per capita expenditures for each service category by the existing population to determine the cost increase assignable to the new nonresidential facility for each service. Total the expenditure increases for each service category to obtain the aggregate assignable costs.	*Public safety cost increase* = *Dollar increase in per capita public costs* × *Existing municipal population* $3,919 = $0.244933 × 16,000 (See Exhibit 10, column 9 for calculations for other public services.)

EXHIBIT 10

EXAMPLE FISCAL IMPACT COST PROJECTION USING THE EMPLOYMENT ANTICIPATION METHOD

USING THE EMPLOYMENT ANTICIPATION METHOD TO EVALUATE THE FISCAL IMPACT OF A DEVELOPMENT PROPOSAL

	STEP 1 Determine Per Capita Municipal Expenditures Column 1	STEP 2 Determine Number of Expected Employees Column 2	STEP 3 Choose Appropriate Per Capita Change Per Employee Column 3	Column 4	STEP 4 Multiply by Number of Employees Column 5	Column 6	STEP 5 Multiply by Existing Per Capita Expenditures Column 7	Column 8	STEP 6 Multiply by Existing Population Column 9
General Government	$\frac{\$236,800}{16,000}$ = $14.80	100,000 FT² NLA	General Government	0.0000018	X 333 = 0.000599		X $14.80 = 0.008865		X 16,000 = $ 142
Public Safety	$\frac{\$726,400}{16,000}$ = $45.40	÷	Public Safety	0.0000162	X 333 = 0.005395		X $45.40 = 0.244933		X 16,000 = $ 3,919
Public Works	$\frac{\$488,000}{16,000}$ = $30.50	1 Employee/ 300 FT²	Public Works	0.0000299	X 333 = 0.009957		X $30.50 = 0.303689		X 16,000 = $ 4,859
Health and Welfare	$\frac{\$22,400}{16,000}$ = $ 1.40	=	Health and Welfare	0.0000104	X 333 = 0.003463		X $ 1.40 = 0.004848		X 16,000 = $ 78
Recreation and Culture	$\frac{\$75,200}{16,000}$ = $ 4.70	333 Employees	Recreation and Culture	0.0000403	X 333 = 0.013420		X $ 4.70 = 0.063074		X 16,000 = $ 1,009
Statutory and Unclassified	$\frac{\$230,400}{16,000}$ = $14.40		Statutory and Unclassified	0.0000496	X 333 = 0.016517		X $14.40 = 0.237845		X 16,000 = $ 3,806
Debt Service	$\frac{\$172,800}{16,000}$ = $10.80		Capital Facilities Debt Service	0.0000212	X 333 = 0.007060		X $10.80 = 0.076248		X 16,000 = $ 1,220
Total			Total Operating and Capital						= $15,033

EXHIBIT 11

EXPENDITURE MULTIPLIERS FOR THE EMPLOYMENT ANTICIPATION METHOD

EXPENDITURE MULTIPLIERS MEASURING THE DEMAND GENERATED IMPACT OF *INDUSTRIAL* ACTIVITY UPON SEVEN CATEGORIES OF PER CAPITA MUNICIPAL EXPENDITURES

City Size	Growing Cities[1] Category of Municipal Service							Declining Cities[1] Category of Municipal Service						
	General Government	Public Safety	Public Works	Health and Welfare	Recreation and Culture	Statutory and Unclassified Expenses	Debt Service	General Government	Public Safety	Public Works	Health and Welfare	Recreation and Culture	Statutory and Unclassified Expenses	Debt Service
Less than 2,500	0.0000022	0.0000181	0.0000337	0.0000465	0.0000518	0.0000925	0.0000607	0.0000161	0.0000564	0.0000689	0.0000280	0.0000182	0.0001042	0.0000380
2,500-4,999	0.0000015	0.0000180	0.0000332	0.0000398	0.0000503	0.0000865	0.0000444	0.0000014	0.0000523	0.0000655	0.0000201	0.0000166	0.0001025	0.0000267
5,000-9,999	0.0000026	0.0000187	0.0000461	0.0000279	0.0000577	0.0000900	0.0000366	0.0000014	0.0000397	0.0000620	0.0000120	0.0000188	0.0001016	0.0000207
10,000-24,999	0.0000018	0.00000162[2]	0.0000299	0.0000104	0.0000403	0.0000496	0.0000212	0.0000008	0.0000168	0.0000471	0.0000033	0.0000006	0.0000540	0.0000136
25,000-49,999	0.0000001	0.0000109	0.0000002	0.0000031	0.0000244	0.0000157	0.0000099	0.0000004	0.0000032	0.0000148	0.0000000	0.0000027	0.0000106	0.0000037
50,000-99,999	0.0000005	0.0000043	0.0000007	0.0000000	0.0000009	0.0000046	0.0000046	0.0000000	0.0000013	0.0000064	00000000	0.0000007	0.0000041	0.0000017
100,000-150,000	0.0000000	0.0000002	0.0000004	0.0000000	0.0000014	0.0000001	0.0000006	0.0000000	0.0000003	0.0000007	0.000000	0.0000006	0.0000007	0.0000004

Notes: 1 Growing and declining cities refer to the direction of population change over the past five to ten years.

2 Numbers are read as fo lows: One additional industrial employee in a growing city whose current population is between 10,000 and 24,999 will increase per capita public safety expenditures by 0.00162 percent.

Source: Rutgers University Center for Urban Policy Research, spring 1977; University of North Carolina (Charlotte), Institute for Urban Studies, 1977.

III. REVENUE PROJECTION TECHNIQUES

FISCAL IMPACT REVENUE PROJECTIONS

Introduction

The U.S. Census Bureau recognizes four major types of revenue sources: general revenue, utility revenue, liquor store revenue, and insurance trust revenue. This *Guide* confines its interest to general revenue because the other sources are not major contributors to a local government's general fund. Utility revenue—the receipts from sales of water, electric service, transit service and gas, is often a large part of a municipality's gross revenues but an insignificant portion of net revenues. User charges (except for transit which is usually a fiscal drain) typically reflect the unit cost of utility operations and do not provide significant local revenue outside the general fund. Similarly, insurance trust revenue, which comes from both contributions from employers and earnings on assets, and which provides income for social insurance and employee retirement benefits usually can be used only to increase the insurance trust fund. Therefore, this type of revenue is also excluded from the discussion. Finally, liquor store revenues (in states that operate public liquor stores) provide such a small proportion of local revenues that they too have been excluded.

Revenues Considered

This *Guide* considers the two primary components of general revenue: (1) *own source revenue,* i.e., raised by the municipality and school district itself and (2) *intergovernmental transfers* contributed to the locality by both the state and Federal governments. The procedural guides in Chapters 9 and 10 of the *Guidebook/Handbook* detail first, how to calculate *own source revenues* including:

taxes — real property, personal property, income sales, property transfer, occupation and business privilege, per capita, transient occupancy.

charges/miscellaneous revenues — interest earnings, fees and permit revenue, fines, forfeitures and penalties.

and second, how to project *intergovernmental transfers* from:

state — sales tax redistribution, income tax distribution, motor fuels tax, cigarette and alcohol tax, educational basic assistance, educational categorical aid, etc.

federal — Revenue Sharing, CDBG, and Federal Impact School Assistance, etc.

Revenue Emphasis

The revenue half of the fiscal impact calculation delves deeply into the array of local fiscal resources. When the user attempts to project revenues, the number of alternative local resources with which he is typically confronted is staggering. Two important segments of information help to mitigate the arduous task of revenue tabulation. The first is a determination of which of these revenues will be impacted by growth. This type of information is included within the narrative of the projection procedure which is demonstrated for each revenue resource in Chapters 9 and 10. Information of this type permits the elimination of several categories of revenue from consideration, making the quantity of revenues with which the analyst must deal more manageable.

More important is a firm grasp by users on how revenues are generated locally. This may be obtained from close scrutinization of local municipal and school district operating budgets. The user will find, for instance, that the locality may depend heavily on the property tax or a locally levied income tax, or for that matter be supported to an extensive degree by intergovernmental transfers, i.e., from either the state or Federal governments. This knowledge of local revenue distribution permits the analyst to segregate those types of revenues which are important and, therefore, must undergo detailed calculations from those which are unimportant, capable of grouping and worthy only of estimation.

Revenue Distribution

Revenue Source	Revenue Most Often Flows Principally To:
I. OWN SOURCE REVENUES	
Property, Income and Sales Taxes	
1. Real Property Tax	Municipality/School District
2. Personal Property Tax	Municipality/School District
3. Income Tax	Municipality/School District
4. Sales Tax	Municipality/School District
Other Taxes	
5. Property Transfer Tax	Municipality/School District
6. Occupation and Business Privilege Tax	Municipality
7. Per Capita Tax	Municipality
8. Transient Occupancy Tax	Municipality
Miscellaneous Revenues	
9. Interest Earnings	Municipality
10. Fees and Permit Revenue	Municipality
11. Fines, Forfeitures and Penalty Revenues	Municipality
User Charges	
12. Recreation, Health and Property Services	Municipality/School District
13. Water, Sewerage and Solid Waste Charges	Municipality

II. INTERGOVERNMENTAL TRANSFERS

State

1. Sales Tax Redistribution	Municipality
2. Income Tax Redistribution	Municipality
3. Motor Fuels Tax Redistribution	Municipality
4. Cigarette and Alcohol Tax Redistribution	Municipality
5. Incorporated/Unincorporated Business Income Tax Redistribution	Municipality
6. Road and Road Lighting Aid	Municipality
7. Public Utilities Franchise Tax Redistribution	Municipality
8. Aid to Urban or Rural Areas	Municipality
9. Homestead and Foregone Tax Rebate	Municipality
10. Educational Basic Support Via Flat Grants	School District
11. Educational Assistance Via Variable Guarantees	School District
12. Educational Categorical Aid	School District
13. Elementary and Secondary Education Act Subsidies (ESEA Titles I-IV)	School District

Federal

14. State/Local Fiscal Assistance Act (Federal Revenue Sharing)	Municipality
15. Community Development Block Grants (CDBG)	Municipality
16. Educational Assistance in Federal Impact Areas (P.L. 815,874)	School District

Source: U.S. Census of Governments, 1972.

PROJECTING REVENUES—OWN SOURCE REVENUES—TAXES

Real Property Tax

The real property tax is frequently the most significant source of local revenues. It is a percentage levy on the value of land and improvements. In most states, the municipality and the school district each levy a separate tax, even though a municipality often collects both revenues. The real property tax rate is expressed either in mills (one thousandth of a dollar) or as a dollar amount per hundred dollars of assessed valuation. A rate of forty mills thus equals a local tax rate of $40.00 per thousand or $4.00 per $100 of assessed valuation.

To project revenues from the real property tax, the analyst multiplies the expected assessed valuation by the local tax rate (expressed as a decimal). The local tax rate multiplied by the expected assessed valuation should always produce the same estimate of revenue as the product of the equalized tax rate and the market or true value of the property. Equalization is a process of estimating true value of a property by applying a sales/assessment ratio to its assessed valuation. County or state governments often use this process because local municipalities often assess at different percentages of true values and frequently have dated assessments. In both cases the assessed value of a property is thus less than its true or market value.

Residential Units for Sale (1,000 single-family homes),
Given Assessed Value and Local Tax Rate

Assessed Value/Unit	x	Local Tax Rate	x	No. of Units	=	Total Revenues
Municipality $40,000	x	$0.94/$100	x	1,000	=	$ 376,000
School District $40,000	x	$2.81/$100	x	1,000	=	$1,124,000

Real Property Transfer Tax

Many municipalities levy a tax on the transfer of real property. This tax is often equally shared by municipality and school district. To project revenues from this source, the analyst multiplies the unit's sales price or market value by the transfer tax rate, the number of units, and the average frequency of unit transfer. A common mistake is to ignore the turnover factor and credit too large a revenue to the development as a result of applying the transfer tax rate to all new units rather than to the estimated annual portion of these units that will change ownership. The turnover figure in the example below is based on 1972 Census data, which indicate that, in general, homeowners move once every five years. Put another way, 20 percent of the owner-occupied housing stock is transferred annually.

Residential (1,000 single-family homes)

Market/Value Unit	x	Transfer Tax Rate	x	No. of Units	x	Percent of Housing Turnover/Year	=	Total Revenues
$50,000	x	.0100	x	1,000	x	.020 (National Figure)	=	$100,000

Sales Tax

As of 1977, 26 states imposed locally levied sales taxes. The tax most often applies to tangible personal property at the rate of 1 percent of the retail sales price. The tax is almost exclusively a source of municipal revenue, except in Louisiana, where school districts are also allowed to tax consumer durables.

Revenue from the local sales tax may be estimated for the new residential development as follows:

Residential Development

New Development
Aggregate Family Income

Income Pre-Development Local Aggregate Family Income	x	Current Revenues from Local Sales	x	Resident Proportion of Total Local Sales*	=	Additional for Local Sales Tax Attributable to Growth
$ 30,000,000 or .15 $200,000,000	x	$200,000	x	.25	=	$7,500

*This information may be obtained from comparable existing facilities in this area.

Per Capita Tax

The per capita tax is a lump sum tax levied on adults aged 18 to 65. It may be levied by municipalities and/or school districts. Revenues derived from new development are estimated by first subtracting dwelling unit estimates of pre-school and school-age children from similar estimates of total household size (HHS). This figure, the estimate of adult resident population, is multiplied by the per capita tax and by the number of anticipated occupied dwelling units.

Earned Income Tax

A significant number of localities throughout the country levy a tax on earned income. The levy is usually shared by municipalities and school districts. Typically the levy is on resident family *earned* income, without allowances for deductions. To project revenues from this source, the most frequent procedure is to convert estimated monthly housing costs (taxes, debt service, and insurance) or contract rental costs to family income. This procedure assumes that a family spends a given percentage of its monthly income on housing. The analyst then multiplies family income by the local income tax rate and the number of units in the development to estimate total revenue from this source.

PROJECTING REVENUES—OWN SOURCE REVENUES
USER CHARGES/MISCELLANEOUS REVENUE
Interest Earnings

Nationally, for units of local government, the largest single category of miscellaneous revenues is interest on investments. Many states allow municipalities to invest a share of their unused revenues during fertile cash flow periods (immediately after taxes are collected) in short-term marketable securities.

As population increases, general revenues increase and more tax-money is available for investment. The per capita amount of revenues resulting from investment remains essentially the same, however. The reverse is also true. As a city begins to decline, the tax base diminishes; the city is not able to issue as many tax anticipation notes and instead must rely on its own cash revenues for lean periods, thus limiting short-term investment potential. The per capita amount also remains relatively constant. The additional revenue resulting from interest on investment may be projected as follows:

Residential (1,000 single-family homes)

Current Estimate of Annual Interest on Earnings, Public Property Rentals and Sales*		*Total Assessed Valuation of the New Development***		*Increment on Investment on Earnings Attributable to Growth*
	x	*Total Assessed Valuation of all Local Properties*	*=*	
$90,000		$ 40,000,000		
		$200,000,000		
$90,000	x	0.20	=	$18,000

* These additional revenues may be lumped in this category for estimation purposes.
** Minus the value of the assessment on the existing vacant land.

Fees and Permits

Most revenue fees and permits are the result of building, occupancy, electrical, explosive and landfill permissions or assurances. Revenue accruing from this source can be estimated via a two step process. First, the current total annual revenue from this source is divided by the current estimate of the number of local dwelling units. Multiplying this figure by the estimated number of incoming dwelling units yields a projection of future development generated revenue from fees and permits.

Fines, Forfeitures and Penalties

Fines are levied locally for violation of traffic, safety (fire), building code and health ordinances. Penalties include payments for tax and library fund delinquency. This revenue resource is almost exclusively a municipal one. It may be estimated on a per capita basis as shown in the following example:

Residential (1,000 single-family homes)

Total Annual Revenues Collected from Fines and Forfeitures	÷	*Current Estimated Population*	=	*Per Capita Revenue from Fines and Forfeitures*
$64,000	÷	$16,000	=	$4.00

Per Capita Revenue from Fines and Forfeitures		*Anticipated Development x Population*		*Total Revenue from = Fines and Forfeitures Attributable to Growth*
$4.00	x	4,300	=	$17,200

User Charges for Water, Sewerage and Sanitation Services

Contrary to the Census definition, municipalities frequently provide water, sewerage, and sanitation services which are neither operated as a distinct segregable authority (in which costs are assumed to equal revenues and thus the general treasury is unaffected) nor are they privately operated (again the assumption is that the general treasury remains unchanged). Frequently a municipality provides water, sewerage and sanitation services using public works personnel and the taxes levied or flat fees charged enter the general treasury. The example below pertains to such a case.

Water and Sewerage

Daily Water Consumption by Type of Facility (gallons/day)		*Number of Days*		*Number of Dwelling Units*	*Total Annual Water = Consumption for Domestic Purpose (gallons)*
250 (single-family homes)	x	365	x	1,000	= 91,250,000
200 (apartments)	x	365	x	500	= 36,500,000

Total Annual Water Consumption	Water Rates + x Sewer Rates	Total Revenue from = Water and Sewerage Charges Attributable to Growth
91,250,000	x $1.50/1,000 Gal.+ .50/1,000 Gal.	= $182,500
36,500,000	x $1.50/1,000 Gal.+ .50/1,000 Gal.	= $ 73,000

PROJECTING REVENUES—INTERGOVERNMENTAL TRANSFERS—STATE

State-Levied Sales Tax Redistribution

Sales tax levied by a state for the privilege of selling or renting tangible personal property at retail rates typically is returned to local governments as a flat and uniform percentage of the locality's taxable retail sales. The reapportionment rate is frequently less than 10 percent of total state taxes collected in a locality. This revenue flows almost exclusively to the general fund of municipalities. The key to predicting additional revenue from this source is to project the additional sales which will take place in the locality. Patterns of the new population's convenience and nonconvenience goods (or shopping goods) purchases and the proportions of income new residents will spend on taxable items in each of these categories are the basic data necessary for the calculation.

Several studies have documented that the great majority of shopping trips by automobile take no more than 7 minutes' travel time (one way) for convenience goods nor 15 minutes for shopping goods. Consumer surveys report that, on average, residents commit 75 percent of their expenditures for convenience goods to local vendors (local is defined as within the area covered by the seven-minute shopping trip) but only 25 percent of their expenditures for shopping goods to local vendors. In addition, according to the Bureau of Labor Statistics, approximately 20 percent of family income is spent on convenience goods and approximately 10 percent on shopping goods. Other studies have estimated that, nationally, approximately 50 percent of consumer expenditures for convenience goods are for taxable goods; approximately 90 percent of consumer expenditures for shopping goods are for taxable items.

To calculate the state sales tax redistribution requires four steps. The analyst must first estimate the new increment of gross sales. From this figure, the analyst must then project the dollar amount of locally captured sales. Third, the analyst applies a tax rate. This figure, times the state-calculated or legislated reapportionment percentage, yields the state redistributed sales tax increment to the locality. The calculation for a development of 1,000 single-family homes is as follows:

Residential (1,000 single-family homes)

New Development Aggregate Family Income	x	Percentage Spent on Goods	=	Amount Spent on Goods
$30,000,000	x	0.20 (convenience)	=	$6,000,000
	x	0.10 (shopping)	=	$3,000,000

Amount Spent on Goods	x	*Taxable Share*	=	*Taxable Share of Goods*
$6,000,000	x	0.50 (convenience)	=	$3,000,000
$3,000,000	x	0.90 (shopping)	=	$2,700,000

Value of Taxable Convenience Goods	x	*Percentage Captured Locally*	=	*Value of Taxable Goods Purchased Locally*
$3,000,000	x	0.75	=	$2,250,000

Value of Taxable Shopping Goods	x	*Percentage Captured Locally*	=	*Value of Taxable Goods Purchased Locally*
$2,700,000	x	0.25	=	$675,000

Value of Taxable Goods Purchased Locally (Convenience plus Shopping)	x	*Sales Tax Rate*	=	*Sales Tax Amount Sent to State*
$2,925,000	x	0.05		$146,250

Sales Tax Amount Sent to State	x	*Legislated or State Determined Percentage of Local Return*	=	*Additional State Sales Tax Revenues Flowing to the Locality*
$146,250		0.10		$14,625

State Income Tax Redistribution

Several states redistribute state-levied income tax to local jurisdictions. In most cases, the direct fiscal flow is to the municipality rather than to the school district. The local reapportionment formula in the majority of cases is based strictly on the proportion of state population and seldom bears any relation to the amount of taxes collected locally. The analyst must remember certain important aspects about any redistribution formula which does not relate to a percentage share of revenues paid directly by the locality to the state but rather distributes "pool" of revenues according to an ever changing share of population, road miles or other criteria: (1) the gross amount of money to be apportioned is changing; (2) other localities within the state are changing their demands on the overall amount via population and/or apportionment criteria variations; and (3) changes in population and/or other apportionment criteria are taking place within the locality other than the development itself.

Practitioner's Notes

(1) Emphasize the importance of the analyst checking *current* entitlement guidelines and funding formulas of the intergovernmental aid programs as these guidelines/ formulas are often modified.

(2) Note that intergovernmental revenues are often more difficult to project than own-source funds: the allocation formulas are more complicated; eligibility for assistance changes as local wealth, unemployment or other indicators move upward or downward; and there are frequent overall community effects that must be considered. (Overall community changes are most likely with annexations and large projects as opposed to smaller scale growth.)

PROJECTING REVENUES—INTERGOVERNMENTAL TRANSFERS—FEDERAL

State-Local Fiscal Assistance Act of 1973 (Federal Revenue Sharing)
Public Law 92-512; 86 Stat 919

The Treasury Department administers funds authorized by this Act. Funds are allocated directly to states and units of local government. Allocation of funds to local governments (two-thirds of the total collected) is based on the local government population, multiplied by the general tax effort (adjusted taxes collected divided by aggregate personal income), multiplied by the relative income factor (per capita income for the local government divided by the per capita income for the county-municipality). Those municipalities with more people, more tax money per dollar of personal income, and larger shares of impoverished residents will receive more money. (No jurisdiction in a state will receive more than 145 percent of the state per capita revenue sharing average, however.) The impact of a large development on revenue sharing funds for a large city is comparatively small. For annexations, border changes, significant rezonings or changes in land use, the detailed calculations may prove worthwhile; for most developments, per capita estimates based on the prior year's allocation may be much more reasonable.

If the analyst wishes to use the detailed calculation, he/she must first estimate current local revenue sharing funds. To do so, the analyst multiplies the latest estimate of the aggregate statewide revenue-sharing funds to be apportioned locally by the locality's ratio (relative to state averages) of population, tax effort, and per capita income. The analyst then projects the amount of locally received revenue-sharing funds resulting from growth. To project this amount, the analyst multiplies the most current estimate of the local amount of revenue-sharing funds by the growth's ratio (relative to local averages) of population, tax effort, and per capita income. The example below illustrates the procedure for a city annexing an area of 45,000 people.

Information on the current estimate of statewide federal revenue-sharing funds to be distributed to localities is available from the state treasurer's office. Some states have developed a simple, iterative computer program which allows state finance personnel to gauge local changes in revenue sharing as a function of annual changes in indices of local entitlement. Several states distribute to municipalities an estimate of all future intergovernmental transfers in November of each year to be used in budget calculations for the following March. This information (relative population, wealth, tax effort, etc.) is often available from the state treasurer's office.

Example Calculations for Federal Revenue-Sharing

Residential (annexation)

Current Estimate of Statewide Federal Revenue-Sharing Funds to be Distributed to Localities		*New Local Population (Including Annexed Area)* / *New State Population*		*New Local Tax Effort (Including Annexed Area)* / *New State Tax Effort*		*New State per Capita Income* / *New Local per Capita Income (Including Annexed Area)*		*Total Local Revenues from Federal Revenue-Sharing Funds*

$$\$40{,}000{,}000 \quad \times \frac{415{,}000}{8{,}300{,}000} \times \frac{0.5}{0.4} \times \frac{\$4{,}350}{\$5{,}000}$$

$$\$40{,}000{,}000 \quad \times \quad .050 \quad \times \quad 1.250 \quad \times \quad .870 \quad = \quad \$2{,}175{,}000$$

Current Estimate of Local Revenue Sharing		*Annexed Area's Population* / *New Local Population (Including Annexed Area)*		*Annexed Area's Tax Effort* / *New Local Tax Effort (Including Annexed Area)*		*New Local per Capita Income (Including Annexed Area)* / *Annexed Area's Per Capita Income*		*Total Local Revenues from Revenue Sharing Attributable to Growth*

$$\$2{,}175{,}000 \ \times \frac{45{,}000 \text{ or } .108}{415{,}000} \times \frac{\$5{,}000 \text{ or } .63}{\$8{,}000}$$

$$\$2{,}175{,}000 \qquad\qquad\qquad\qquad \times \quad .0351 \qquad = \$76{,}343$$

Educational Assistance in Federal Impact Areas—
Public Law 81-874; 64 Stat 1100

This subsidy, commonly called impact aid, is given to "local educational agencies upon which the United States has placed financial burdens." The analyst should check with the local school district superintendent and the state department of education (federal grants office) to help determine how many children in the housing being constructed are likely to qualify for impact aid. Federal impact aid per pupil typically equals the per student revenue derived from local sources in a comparable nonimpacted district. Impact aid per pupil times the number of children qualifying for impact aid equals the projected revenue from this source.

Practitioner's Notes

(1) Check the local budget to determine the presence and relative importance of the different federal intergovernmental revenues. Allocate time for projecting revenues accordingly.

(2) Check current program entitlement guidelines and funding formulas.

(3) Intergovernmental revenues are often more difficult to project than own-source funds: the allocation formulas are more complicated; eligibility for assistance changes as local wealth, unemployment or other indicators move upward or downward; and there are frequent overall community effects that must be considered.

IV. RELATED INFORMATION— LEGAL, MODELS, MULTIPLIERS

FISCAL IMPACT—LEGAL CLIMATE AND COMPUTERIZED MODELS

LEGAL CLIMATE

Background

Fiscal impact considerations are either legally authorized or there are fertile grounds for authorization within the confines of numerous planning or planning related tasks. Economy and efficiency in the land development process have long been basic planning objectives. Fiscal impact calculations could thus easily be a part of a comprehensive planning process.

Fiscal impact analysis further can be used in cases of special exception or permitting use (for instance, as part of the PUD approval process) to assure local fiscal stability throughout the multiple stages of a large development. It may be used in variances or rezonings to provide documentation that undue hardship to an individual property owner is mitigated by general community economic benefit or that the fiscal situation has so changed in a community that the existing zoning bears no relationship to reality and, in fact, is counterproductive to orderly growth.

Fiscal impact considerations are similarly useful in annexations. They assess the likely financial outcome of convergence to both jurisdictions and prevent annexations which would be especially beneficial to the residents of one jurisdiction at the expense of the residents of the other.

Yet the user must realize, however, that every land use cannot be a municipal benefit, and while we may assess relative fiscal merit, it does not follow that those land uses that either are not as beneficial as others or impose a liability can then necessarily be excluded.

Where fiscal impact analysis has had some history, the courts have in part specified its role. Fiscal considerations, while the concern of local land use policy, are neither the sole concern, nor may they be the basis on which to exclude totally a category of land use. The courts have indicated that localities may use this information to plan for the future; however, the fiscal implications of particular development are only one element within the planning process. Courts have recognized that municipalities also have to provide housing for those who work nearby, answer regional as well as local needs, and provide housing opportunities for those who are economically or racially disadvantaged.

Practitioner's Notes

(1) Jurisdictions with the most experience in fiscal impact analysis frequently have the largest representation in the case law. However as fiscal impact analysis becomes a part of the planning process it has a tendency to be misused to permanently or totally exclude a category of land use because of its "negative" fiscal impact. This will be reacted to harshly by the courts. Exclusion need not be the outcome of a negative impact analysis. One may look to pair a more costly land use with concurrent or future less costly development. A negative analysis may be further used to gauge future revenue raising requirements.

COMPUTERIZED MODELS

Background

Fiscal impact analyses are often time consuming. After completing an initial analysis the planner typically is faced with repeating the entire process should he desire to calculate either variations of a specific proposal or alternative growth strategies. The necessity to increase speed of computations and the desire for a more rigorous approach to fiscal impact analysis have led to the rise of cost-revenue models for computers. Since most calculations are routine and repetitive they lend themselves to computer use.

In addition to simplifying the task of performing sensitivity analysis, computer models usually have the capacity to store information such that the cumulative effect of historical development decisions becomes a part of each current fiscal impact analysis. For example, assume that a community has recently adopted a planned unit development (PUD) ordinance. Several development proposals are received, each containing multiple housing types and each having a specific fiscal impact on the community. Most computerized fiscal impact approaches are able to assess the impact of each development on the local fisc serially—taking into account the fiscal effects of previous developments. Further, it is possible through computerized approaches to view the impact of multiple proposals. Thus the impact of a development 70 percent completed may be viewed simultaneously with one 25 percent completed.

Computerized models are an important part of fiscal impact analysis. They simplify the tasks of county, regional and state agencies that must review locally submitted fiscal impact statements. They can provide small municipalities with quick and sophisticated analysis of a specific development. If used judiciously, models may become an intricate part of the everyday planning analysis performed in larger cities or counties where rapid growth is occurring or areas where there is a desire for more intensive econometric analysis than is currently available.

Practitioner's Notes

(1) Point out to users the considerable data gathering which must be undertaken prior to setting up the model. This is often many, many times the effort required to conduct a single fiscal impact analysis. Model employment should thus reflect a need for numerous fiscal impact analyses in a single jurisdiction or a desire for significant sensitivity analysis of a more limited set of development, zone change or annexation alternatives.

(2) Most models are arithmetic—a few econometric. The latter, more sophisticated and more "black box," often make it more difficult to convey the results of an analysis to the public.

(3) Model services from proprietors are usually available with ongoing consulting for both data gathering and analysis phases.

DEMOGRAPHIC MULTIPLIERS IN FISCAL IMPACT ANALYSIS

Background (See Section VI for updated multipliers)

Demographic multipliers are used to predict the municipal and school populations that will result from new housing development. When the number, type and configuration of incoming housing units and therefore the magnitude of the new population are known, estimates of public service requirements and costs (i.e., police, fire, public works, personnel/equipment, etc.) can easily be projected. The multipliers which describe the two principal users of local services (people for municipal services and school-age children for school services) are frequently expressed by number of rooms or bedrooms. The example below illustrates such multipliers.

Demographic Characteristics	Single-Family Homes Number of Bedrooms			Garden Apartments Number of Bedrooms	
Northeast/New England	Two	Three	Four	One	Two
Total household size*	2.485	3.940	4.965	1.500	2.430
School-age children	0.246	1.130	2.068	0.038	0.150

* Total household size is the total number of persons, both related and unrelated, residing in a housing unit. School-age children includes all persons aged 5 to 18 residing in the housing unit.

These multipliers are developed from household surveys or from data found in the U.S. Census Public Use Samples for recently constructed housing. The example above is interpreted: "An average of 3.94 residents and 1.13 school-age children live in a three-bedroom, single-family home in New England. An average of 1.50 residents and 0.038 school-age children are found to live in one-bedroom garden apartments in the same area. If three-bedroom, single-family homes or one-bedroom, garden apartments are proposed to be developed locally, the product of demographic multipliers and the number of forthcoming housing units provides an estimate of the magnitude of new residents and school-age children for whom municipal and school services must be provided.

Assume, for example, that one hundred, one bedroom garden apartments are being considered for an area. Assume also that locally it costs $200 per person to provide municipal (general government, public safety, public works, health/welfare, recreation) services and $2,000 per pupil to provide school (primary and secondary education) services. Using the demographic multipliers shown above, one hundred, one bedroom garden apartments would, on the average, generate 150 people (1.500 x 100) and four school-age children (.038 x 100). Multiplying these population estimates by per capita and per pupil servicing costs indicates that roughly $38,000 will be the cost to provide public services to the new apartments (150 x $200) plus (4 x $2,000).

Calculating Demographic Multipliers

Until recently practitioners have depended on demographic multipliers determined from local field surveys to project future population. Often sample sizes, procedures, specific characteristics of occupants, etc., allowed the results of the surveys to be applicable in only limited areas. One of the larger samples was a 1973 Rutgers University survey—results were reported for four structure types (garden apartments, high-rise apartments, single-family homes and townhouses). The *Handbook/Guide* draws largely on the methods and instruments used in this survey and explains how and when to sample for demographic multipliers. It covers such matters as questionnaire design, sample size, survey efficiency, and survey costs. It further lists basic references for undertaking survey research. Due to the cost and complexity of survey sampling, the practitioner should definitely consult these sources before planning a field survey to determine demographic characteristics.

A better procedure for determining demographic multipliers has also begun to emerge, however. This procedure uses U.S. Census Public Use Samples to estimate demographic multipliers by housing type. The analyst can obtain an appropriate state or county group Census tape for an area, use certain programming to define housing tapes and convert age group distributions to school-age children, and thus estimate the number of people and pupils by housing type. Due to the rising costs of sample surveys and the possibility of bias due to sample design or administration, employment of the U.S. Census Public Use Samples is receiving increasing attention. The *Handbook/Guidebook* provides definitions and procedures for calculating multipliers via the Public Use Sample.

Practitioner's Notes

(1) Discuss the definitions of total household size and school-age children. Be sure to distinguish between school-age children and *public* school-age children.
(2) Discuss studies involving regional and temporal variation of demographic multipliers. Emphasize that lack of temporal variation does not hold for the post-1970 period.
(3) Point out how demographic multipliers can be tallied and the advantages/disadvantages of both local survey sampling and the national Public Use Sample.
(4) Cover the historical evolution of demographic multipliers and the studies which have led them to be presented in their current format.

V. HYPOTHETICAL PROBLEMS AND SOLUTIONS

PROJECTING COSTS: HYPOTHETICAL PROBLEMS FOR EACH METHOD

Per Capita Multiplier Method Hypothetical Problem

A 100 unit single-family development is proposed in a Pennsylvania community of 10,000 residents and 2,500 public school pupils. Twenty percent of the proposed single-family homes will be two bedroom units. The community spends the following amounts for public services:

MUNICIPAL			*SCHOOL DISTRICT*	
Operating			Operating	$4,500,000
General Government	$	150,000	Debt Service	500,000
Public Safety		500,000	Total	$5,000,000
Public Works		500,000		
Health & Welfare		120,000		
Recreation & Culture		80,000		
Debt Service		150,000		
Total		$1,500,000		

What impact will the 100 unit development have on municipal and school district expenditures? (Assume for calculation purposes that: (1) all children from the development will attend public schools; and (2) that $300,000 of the $1,500,000 municipal expenditure is occasioned by local nonresidential uses.)

Answer

Development generated municipal costs:	*$ 46,560*
Development generated school district costs	*252,000*
Total	*$298,560*

Service Standard Method Hypothetical Problem

A 200 unit townhouse development is proposed in a Texas community of 30,000 residents and 10,000 public school pupils. Forty percent of the townhouses are two bedroom units and sixty percent are three bedroom units. The community has the following annual operating costs for different public service employees.

Public Service Functions	Operating Cost Per Employee
MUNICIPAL	
GENERAL GOVERNMENT	
Financial Administration	$16,000
General Control	13,500
PUBLIC SAFETY	
Police	20,000
Fire	18,000
PUBLIC WORKS	
Highways	18,000
Sewerage	15,000
Sanitation	14,000
Water Supply	14,000
RECREATION AND CULTURE	
Parks and Recreation	12,000
Libraries	13,500
SCHOOL DISTRICT	
Primary and Secondary School	20,000

What impact will the 200 unit development have on municipal and school district expenditures? (Assume that 90 percent of the development's school-age children will attend public schools.)

Answer

Development generated municipal costs:	*$117,183*
Development generated school district costs:	*277,907*
Total	*$395,090*

Comparable City Method Hypothetical Problem

A 1,000 unit single-family development is proposed in an Oregon community. In 1970, the locality had a population of 5,000 residents and 1,500 public school pupils; in 1979, 7,500 residents and 1,900 pupils. The community has the following expenditures:

Public Service Functions	Total Operating Costs	Total Capital Costs
MUNICIPAL		
General Government	$ 84,000	$ 8,000
Public Safety	480,000	60,000
Public Works	600,000	70,000
Health & Welfare	12,000	7,000
Recreation & Culture	24,000	5,000
SCHOOL DISTRICT		
Primary and Secondary Schools	$3,420,000	$300,000

What impact will the development have on municipal and school district expenditures? (Assume that 90 percent of the development's school-age children attend public schools and that construction takes 2 years.)

Answer

Development generated municipal costs:	*$1,309,571*
Development generated school district costs:	*2,243,040*
Total	*$3,552,611*

Proportional Valuation Method Hypothetical Problem

A 100,000 ft.² industrial facility is proposed in a locality with the following financial characteristics:

Municipal expenditures:	$ 4,000,000
Total local real property value:	$200,000,000
Total nonresidential real property value:	$ 70,000,000
Total number of parcels:	11,000
Total number of nonresidential parcels:	900

What impact will the industrial facility have on municipal expenditures? (Assume the facility has an estimated $2,000,000 real property value.)

Answer

Development generated municipal costs:	*$12,180*

Employment Anticipation Method Hypothetical Problem

A 300,000 ft.² factory that will employ 1,000 workers is proposed in a growing community of 10,000 residents. The community has the following municipal expenditures:

General Government	$150,000	Health & Welfare	$ 12,500
Public Safety	462,500	Recreation & Culture	37,500
Public Works	350,000	Statutory & Unclassfd.	187,500
		Capital Facilities/	
		Debt Services	100,000

What impact will the factory have on municipal expenditures?

Answer

Development generated municipal costs:	*$31,289*

PER CAPITA MULTIPLIER METHOD—SOLUTION TO HYPOTHETICAL PROBLEM

	Number of Dwelling Units (1)	Demographic Multipliers Household (2)	Students (2)	Total Residents[1] (3)	Students[1] (3)	Annual Expenditures Per Capita Municipal[2] (4)	Annual Expenditures Per Pupil School District[2] (4)	Total Annual Expenditures Municipal[4] (5)	Total Annual Expenditures School District[4] (5)	Total Annual Public (Municipal and School District) Expenditures (6)
Single Family Homes (100)										
2 bedroom	20	2.536	0.288	51	6	$120	$2,000	$ 6,120	$ 12,000	$ 18,120
3 bedroom	40	3.776	1.111	151	44	120	2,000	18,120	88,000	106,120
4 bedroom	40	4.655	1.911	186	76	120	2,000	22,320	152,000	174,320
Total	100	—	—	388	126[3]	—	—	46,560	252,000	298,560

Notes: 1 Equals the demographic multipliers shown in column (2) multiplied by the number of units shown in column (1).
2 Includes operating and debt service for capital facilities.
3 Calculation assumes that all school age children attend public schools.
4 Equals total residents/students multiplied by cost per resident/student.

STATE DISTRIBUTION BY REGION AND SUBREGION

REGIONS:

NORTHEAST — *Connecticut, Maine, Massachusetts, New Hampshire, New Jersey, New York, Pennsylvania, Rhode Island, Vermont.*

NORTH CENTRAL — *Illinois, Indiana, Iowa, Kansas, Michigan, Minnesota, Missouri, Nebraska, North Dakota, Ohio, South Dakota, Wisconsin.*

SOUTH — *Alabama, Arkansas, Delaware, Florida, Georgia, Kentucky, Louisiana, Maryland, Mississippi, North Carolina, Oklahoma, South Carolina Tennessee, Texas, Virginia, Washington, D.C., West Virginia.*

WEST — *Alaska, Arizona, California, Colorado, Hawaii, Idaho, Montana, Nevada, New Mexico, Oregon, Utah, Washington, Wyoming.*

SUBREGIONS:

NORTHEAST — *New England: Connecticut, Maine, Massachusetts, New Hampshire, Rhode Island, Vermont.*
              Middle Atlantic: New Jersey, New York, Pennsylvania.

NORTH CENTRAL — *East North Central: Illinois, Indiana, Michigan, Ohio, Wisconsin.*
                  West North Central: Iowa, Kansas, Minnesota, Missouri, Nebraska, North Dakota, South Dakota.

SOUTH — *South Atlantic: Delaware, Florida, Georgia, Maryland, North Carolina, South Carolina, Virginia, West Virginia.*
          East South Central: Alabama, Kentucky, Mississippi, Tennessee.
          West South Central: Arkansas, Louisiana, Oklahoma, Texas.

WEST — *Mountain: Arizona, Colorado, Idaho, Montana, Nevada, New Mexico, Utah, Wyoming.*
         Pacific: Alaska, California, Hawaii, Oregon, Washington.

SERVICE STANDARD METHOD—SOLUTION TO HYPOTHETICAL PROBLEM

		Step 2	Step 2	Step 3	Step 4	Step 5	Step 5	Step 6
Step 1	Step 1	Manpower Ratios for Population Size Group and Region[2]	Estimated Number of Future Employees[3]	Operating Expenses Per Future Employee[4]	Total Annual Operating Costs by Function[5]	Capital-to-Operating Ratios for Population Size Group and Region[6]	Total Annual Capital Costs by Function[7]	Total Annual Public Costs (Operating + Capital) by Function[8]
Anticipated Population and Public School-Age Children[1] (1)	Governmental Functions (2)	(3)	(4)	(5)	(6)	(7)	(8)	(9)
666 Population (166 Public-School-age Children)	**MUNICIPAL FUNCTIONS**							
	General Government							
	Finance Administration	.52	.35	$16,000	$ 5,600	.008	$ 45	$ 5,645
	General Control	.53	.35	13,500	4,725	.008	38	4,763
200 Townhouses (80 two-bedroom; 120 three bedroom)	Public Safety							
	Police	2.01	1.34	20,000	26,800	.051	1,367	28,167
	Fire	1.64	1.09	18,000	19,620	.022	432	20,052
	Public Works							
	Highways	1.00	.67	18,000	12,060	.284	3,425	15,485
	Sewerage	.53	.35	15,000	5,250	.345	1,811	7,061
	Sanitation	1.44	.96	14,000	13,440	.064	860	14,300
	Water Supply	.99	.66	14,000	9,240	.386	3,567	12,807
	Recreation and Culture							
	Parks and Recreation	.82	.55	12,000	6,600	.124	818	7,418
	Libraries	.17	.11	13,500	1,485	.000	—	1,485
	Total Municipal				104,820		12,363	117,183
	SCHOOL DISTRICT							
	Primary/Secondary Schools	78.00	12.95	20,000	259,000	.073	18,907	277,907
	Total School District				259,000		18,907	277,907
	TOTAL MUNICIPAL AND SCHOOL DISTRICT				$363,820		$ 31,270	$395,090

Notes:

1. Use demographic multipliers for Southern Region, West South Central Subregion. Ten percent of all school-age children attend private schools.
2. Use service standards for Southern communities of 25,000 to 49,999 population.
3. Anticipated population (666) and (166) public school-age children (expressed in 000s as .666 and .166 respectively) multiplied by service ratios as shown in column 3.
4. Determined by dividing total operating costs for each service function by total public employees per service function.
5. Column 4 multiplied by column 5.
6. Use capital-to-operating expenditure ratios for Southern communities of 25,000 to 49,999 population.
7. Column 6 multiplied by column 7.
8. Column 6 plus column 8.

COMPARABLE CITY METHOD—SOLUTION TO HYPOTHETICAL PROBLEM

Step 1 — Anticipated Increments of Population and School-Age Children (1): 3,826 Population[1]; 1,130 School-Age Children (Public)

Governmental Functions (2)	Current Expenditure Multipliers[2] Op (3)	Cap (3)	Future Expenditure Multipliers Op[3] (4)	Cap (4)	Future-Current Exp. Multiplier Ratio Op (5)	Cap (5)	Current Annual Exp. per Person/Pupil Op (6)	Cap (6)	Future Annual Exp.[4] per Person/Pupil Op (7)	Cap (7)	Future Total Annual Exp. Op (8)	Cap (8)	Current Total Annual Exp. Op (9)	Cap (9)	Net Annual Cost by Function Op (10)	Cap (10)	Total Operating and Capital Costs
MUNICIPAL																	
General government	0.81	0.25	0.86	0.49	1.06	1.96	$11.20	$1.07	$11.87	$2.40	$134,440	$23,785	$84,000	$8,000	$50,440	$15,785	$66,225
Public safety	0.62	1.08	0.82	1.00	1.32	.93	64.00	8.00	84.48	7.44	956,820	84,265	480,000	60,000	476,820	24,265	501,085
Public works	1.05	0.60	1.05	0.75	1.00	1.25	80.00	9.33	80.00	11.66	906,080	132,061	600,000	70,000	306,080	62,061	368,141
Health and Welfare	0.04	0.40	0.58	0.83	14.50	2.08	1.60	.93	23.20	1.93	262,763	21,859	12,000	7,000	250,763	14,859	265,622
Recreation and Culture	0.44	0.05	0.64	0.56	1.45	11.20	3.20	.67	4.64	7.50	52,533	84,945	24,000	5,000	28,553	79,945	108,498
																TOTAL MUNICIPAL	**$1,309,571**
SCHOOL DISTRICT																	
Primary/Secondary Schools	0.99	1.05	1.00	1.00	1.01	.95	$1800.00	$158.00	$1,818.00	$150.00	$5,508,540	$454,500	$3,420,000	$300,000	$2,088,540	$154,500	$2,243,040
																TOTAL MUNICIPAL AND SCHOOL DISTRICT	**$3,552,611**

Notes:

1. Use blended multipliers for Western region, Pacific subregion. Calculation assumes that 90 percent of all school-age children attend public schools.
2. Use multipliers for communities between 1,000 and 10,000 population with an annual growth rate above 2 percent.
3. Use multipliers for communities between 10,000 and 24,999 population with an annual growth rate above 2 percent.
4. Equals future per capita operating/capital cost multiplied by future total population (11,326 residents—7,500 current population plus 3,826 residents introduced by 1,000 unit single-family development) and future public school pupils (3,030 pupils—1,900 current pupils plus 1,130 students introduced by the development).

PROPORTIONAL VALUATION METHOD—SOLUTION TO HYPOTHETICAL PROBLEM

LOCAL NONRESIDENTIAL USE COST PROJECTION   (Step 2)

Total Existing Municipal Expenditures Attributable to Nonresidential Uses	=	Total Municipal Expenditures	X	Proportion of Nonresidential Value to Total Local Real Property Value[1]	X	Refinement Coefficient[2]
		$4,000,000	X	($\frac{\$\ 70,000,000}{\$200,000,000}$	X	1.20)
$1,680,000	=	$4,000,000	X	(.35	X	1.20)

INCOMING NONRESIDENTIAL USE COST PROJECTION   (Step 3)

Municipal Costs Allocated to the Incoming Nonresidential Facility	=	Total Existing Municipal Expenditures Attributable to Nonresidential Uses	X	Proportion of Facility to Total Local Nonresidential Real Property Value[3]	X	Refinement Coefficient[4]
		$1,680,000	X	($\frac{\$\ 2,000,000}{\$70,000,000}$	X	.25)
$12,180	=	$1,680,000	X	(.029	X	.25)

INCOMING NONRESIDENTIAL USE COST DISTRIBUTION   (Step 4)

	Distribution of Total Costs	
	Percentage[5]	Dollars
Municipal Service Category		
General Government	4	$ 731
Public Safety	75	9,135
Public Works	15	1,827
Health and Welfare	2	244
Recreation and Culture	2	244
TOTAL	100	$12,180

1   Simple Proportional Valuation $= \frac{\text{Existing Total Local Nonresidential Real Property Value}}{\text{Total Local Real Property Value}}$

2   The value multiplier for the refinement coefficient (1.20) is determined by comparing the average value of nonresidential parcels ($\frac{\$70,000,000}{900}$ or $77,778) to the average value of all parcels ($\frac{\$200,000,000}{11,000}$ or $18,182).

The relationship of these two values ($\frac{\$77,778}{\$18,182}$ or 4.3) yields the 1.20 refinement coefficient.

3   Simple Proportional Valuation $= \frac{\text{Subject Nonresidential Real Property Value}}{\text{Existing Total Nonresidential Real Property Value}}$

4   The value multiplier for the refinement coefficient (.25) is determined by comparing the value of the new nonresidential facility ($2,000,000) to the average value of local nonresidential parcels ($18,182). The relationship of these two values yields ($\frac{\$2,000,000}{\$\ \ 77,778}$ or 26) yields the .25 refinement coefficient.

5   Determined from local interviews.

EMPLOYMENT ANTICIPATION METHOD—SOLUTION TO HYPOTHETICAL PROBLEM

	Step 1	Step 2	Step 3		Step 4		Step 5		Step 6
	Determine Per Capita Municipal Expenditures	Determine Number of Expected Employees	Choose Appropriate Per Capita Change Per Employee		Multiply by Number of Employees		Multiply by Existing Per Capita Expenditures		Multiply by Existing Population
	Column 1	Column 2	Column 3	Column 4	Column 5	Column 6	Column 7	Column 8	Column 9
General Government	$\frac{\$150,000}{10,000}$ = $15.00	300,000 FT² NLA	0.0000018		× 1,000	= 0.001800	× $15.00	= $0.027000	× 10,000 = $ 270
Public Safety	$\frac{\$462,500}{10,000}$ = $46.25	÷	0.0000162		× 1,000	= 0.016200	× $46.25	= 0.749250	× 10,000 = $ 7,493
Public Works	$\frac{\$350,000}{10,000}$ = $35.00	1 Employee/ 300 FT²	0.0000299		× 1,000	= 0.029900	× $35.00	= 1.046500	× 10,000 = $10,465
Health and Welfare	$\frac{\$12,500}{10,000}$ = $ 1.25	=	0.0000104		× 1,000	= 0.010400	× $ 1.25	= 0.013000	× 10,000 = $ 130
Recreation and Culture	$\frac{\$37,500}{10,000}$ = $ 3.75	1,000 Employees	0.0000403		× 1,000	= 0.040300	× $ 3.75	= 0.151125	× 10,000 = $ 1,511
Statutory and Unclassified	$\frac{\$187,500}{10,000}$ = $18.75		0.0000496		× 1,000	= 0.049600	× $18.75	= 0.930000	× 10,000 = $ 9,300
Capital Facilities Debt Service	$\frac{\$100,000}{10,000}$ = $10.00		0.0000212		× 1,000	= 0.021200	× $10.00	= 0.212000	× 10,000 = $ 2,120
Total									
Total Operating and Capital									$31,289

VI.   1980 DEMOGRAPHIC MULTIPLIERS

THE SAMPLE

The multipliers for standard housing types presented here have been derived from information obtained from the *1980 Census of Population and Housing*–Public Use Sample. The Public Use Sample is comprised of computer tapes which contain records for a sample of housing units with information on the characteristics of each unit and the people in it. The Public Use file (5 percent sample) is the basic source of information provided here—size of household (including the number of household members who are of school age) by the size of the dwelling unit they occupy (expressed in terms of the number of bedrooms in the housing unit).

The Public Use Sample is uniquely crafted by the Bureau of Census to provide information to researchers which is not available in standard Census publications or from the published portfolio material of the Summary Tape File. The Public Use Sample permits cross-tabulations by desired variables, i.e., housing occupants by bedroom configuration as well as empirical definitions of housing types. The latter, for instance, allows townhouses to be defined as: single-family attached units of three stories or less, in groups of five units or more.

The sample of housing included here is drawn from recently constructed units (built from 1975 to 1980) monitored in 1980. This is done to approximate local impact conditions after new development takes place. The period of analysis has been narrowed to five years in this presentation from ten years in prior presentations in *The Fiscal Impact Handbook* and *Practitioner's Guide to Fiscal Impact Analysis* to enhance the aspect of immediate impact.

From this sample of new units are removed non-standard or non-arms-length housing unit transfer or tenure relationships. These include cases wherein property is transferred for, or costs of occupancy are, significantly less than normal. This has been achieved by removing from the sample all units in the lowest 10 percent of the value or rent distribution.

Further, cities in excess of 100,000 population have been removed from the survey. New housing in large cities is presumed to contain a substantial amount of publicly subsidized housing and is therefore eliminated. (The Public Use Sample does not allow direct specification of publicly aided housing.)

Finally, adult education has been removed from school counts by grade. A small percentage of adults, mostly residents of single-family homes, attend local public schools in the evening. This is reported in the number of school attendees by grade and can affect school-age children tallies if this sub-population is not eliminated.

TOTAL HOUSEHOLD SIZE (Exhibit 12)

Household size is the number of people occupying a dwelling unit regardless of family relationship. Average household size is the mean number of people found across numerous housing units. An excellent way of remembering the magnitude of household size is that the number of people per household is roughly equivalent to the number of bedrooms in the unit. One-bedroom units on average have 1+ people per unit, two-bedroom units have 2+ people per unit, and four-bedroom units have 4+ people per unit. By housing type, high-rise apartments have the least number of people per given bedroom configuration; mobile homes have the most.

Average household size has declined nationally over the period 1970 to 1980 from 3.14 to 2.75 (which is close to its 1985 level). This decade decline of approximately 12.4 percent has occurred across most housing types and bedroom ranges, yet, not to the same degree. Mobile homes decreased in household size the least of all housing types. In most instances, the decrease was between five and ten percent. The apparent scenario is that the continued high cost of traditionally constructed housing has caused some families to remain longer in mobile homes and also caused other, larger families to seek out this housing form. In the former case, pre-school children became school age; in the latter, families with children move into larger-bedroom mobile units. Both contribute to increasing household size.

The greatest decline in household size took place in townhouses. This occurred for three reasons. First, the cost of these units often limits purchase to dual-income families with delayed child raising. Second, the townhouse configuration is attractive to the elderly because of the reduced maintenance aspects of this form of ownership. Third, when townhouses were originally sampled in 1970 there were very few of them and they were often occupied by the same types of large, family-raising households that would have occupied a single-family home. Today, townhouses have a distinct place in the market, sought often by those who desire less maintenance associated with ownership but more space and privacy than is offered in a garden apartment or condominium. These typically are young or elderly households with fewer children than are found in single-family homes or even in garden apartments.

SCHOOL CHILDREN PROFILE

For the mid-1980s and well into the 1990s, the effects of delayed and reduced child raising will continue to be felt on the number of school children per dwelling unit. This is a well-known fact to demographers who chart a "baby bust" beginning in 1962 and continuing through the current period. The decline in births had initial impact on

EXHIBIT 12

REGIONAL AND NATIONAL DEMOGRAPHIC MULTIPLIERS FOR COMMON CONFIGURATIONS OF STANDARD HOUSING TYPES FOR

TOTAL HOUSEHOLD SIZE

—BY HOUSING TYPE AND NUMBER OF BEDROOMS—
[For housing built during 1975-1980 and monitored in 1980]

REGION	SINGLE FAMILY					GARDEN APARTMENTS				TOWNHOUSE			
	2 BR	3 BR	4 BR	5 BR	Blended (All BRs)	1 BR	2 BR	3 BR	Blended (All BRs)	1 BR	2 BR	3 BR	Blended (All BRs)
NORTHEAST	2.307	3.287	4.061	4.853	3.364	1.390	2.163	3.341	1.856	1.639	2.037	2.833	2.426
New England	2.417	3.345	4.141	4.853	3.325	1.295	2.142	3.074	1.768	1.491	2.098	3.000	2.355
Middle Atlantic	2.223	3.258	4.031	4.853	3.384	1.443	2.175	3.439	1.904	1.695	2.019	2.808	2.441
NORTH CENTRAL	2.381	3.313	4.124	5.082	3.432	1.292	2.029	3.188	1.780	1.422	2.011	2.727	2.353
East North Central	2.340	3.308	4.134	5.084	3.393	1.302	2.031	3.183	1.783	1.466	2.023	2.742	2.385
West North Central	2.429	3.321	4.104	5.080	3.238	1.270	2.025	3.340	1.774	1.342	1.988	2.690	2.286
SOUTH	2.375	3.191	3.953	4.664	3.179	1.445	2.157	3.233	2.071	1.650	2.107	2.702	2.442
South Atlantic	2.301	3.145	3.889	4.618	3.308	1.471	2.092	3.435	2.086	1.751	2.118	2.685	2.491
East South Central	2.455	3.263	4.004	4.592	3.275	1.376	2.123	3.481	2.052	1.434	2.064	2.733	2.287
West South Central	2.459	3.205	4.013	4.855	3.318	1.447	2.287	3.155	2.059	1.575	2.098	2.793	2.314
WEST	2.467	3.170	3.944	4.902	3.399	1.507	2.212	3.317	2.050	1.860	1.996	2.591	2.291
Mountain	2.492	3.246	4.097	5.177	3.272	1.434	2.204	3.099	2.007	1.754	1.886	2.566	2.216
Pacific	2.449	3.127	3.870	4.694		1.533	2.215		2.065	1.885	2.038	2.598	2.316
NATIONAL (All Region Average)	2.390	3.225	4.006	4.861	3.312	1.409	2.138	3.262	1.965	1.670	2.040	2.694	2.377

REGION	HIGH RISE				MOBILE HOMES				DUPLEX, TRIPLEX, QUADPLEX			
	Studio	1 BR	2 BR	Blended (All BRs)	1 BR	2 BR	3 BR	Blended (All BRs)	1 BR	2 BR	3 BR	Blended (All BRs)
NORTHEAST	1.055	1.257	2.072	1.405	1.689	2.193	3.528	2.667	1.492	2.322	3.429	2.527
New England	1.067	1.221	1.956	1.376	1.560	2.127	3.444	2.505	1.398	2.326	3.430	2.350
Middle Atlantic	1.054	1.272	2.129	1.417	1.761	2.217	3.551	2.724	1.556	2.320	3.429	2.619
NORTH CENTRAL	1.034	1.135	1.799	1.258	1.795	2.231	3.393	2.684	1.395	2.134	3.099	2.259
East North Central	1.050	1.126	1.842	1.270	1.750	2.229	3.441	2.658	1.473	2.127	3.093	2.275
West North Central	1.000	1.165	1.600	1.217	1.873	2.235	3.332	2.726	1.305	2.146	3.110	2.233
SOUTH	1.103	1.274	1.917	1.516	2.061	2.391	3.572	2.849	1.695	2.281	3.237	2.472
South Atlantic	1.120	1.330	1.914	1.580	2.027	2.300	3.536	2.759	1.714	2.237	3.228	2.434
East South Central	1.095	1.090	1.800	1.175	2.165	2.544	3.574	2.958	1.584	2.315	3.255	2.502
West South Central	1.000	1.057	2.286	1.200	2.058	2.443	3.623	2.918	1.732	2.342	3.238	2.516
WEST	1.343	1.528	2.218	1.770	1.912	2.151	3.382	2.574	1.927	2.313	3.093	2.513
Mountain	1.000	1.162	1.611	1.253	2.048	2.312	3.495	2.803	1.723	2.360	3.040	2.533
Pacific	1.348	1.607	2.279	1.848	1.825	2.057	3.259	2.408	2.013	2.292	3.114	2.504
NATIONAL (All Region Average)	1.128	1.260	1.989	1.457	1.946	2.286	3.489	2.734	1.643	2.257	3.187	2.439

Source: U.S. Department of Commerce, Bureau of the Census, *U.S. Census of Population and Housing (Public Use Sample),* 1980.

EXHIBIT 13

REGIONAL AND NATIONAL DEMOGRAPHIC MULTIPLIERS FOR COMMON CONFIGURATIONS OF STANDARD HOUSING TYPES FOR SCHOOL-AGE CHILDREN

—BY HOUSING TYPE AND NUMBER OF BEDROOMS—
[For housing built during 1975-1980 and monitored in 1980]

REGION	SINGLE FAMILY					GARDEN APARTMENTS				TOWNHOUSE			
	2 BR	3 BR	4 BR	5 BR	Blended (All BRs)	1 BR	2 BR	3 BR	Blended (All BRs)	1 BR	2 BR	3 BR	Blended (All BRs)
NORTHEAST	.199	.734	1.366	1.955	.845	.017	.231	.857	.175	.038	.164	.550	.377
New England	.243	.793	1.470	2.052	.840	.007	.203	.883	.155	.053	.147	.676	.348
Middle Atlantic	.166	.705	1.328	1.921	.847	.023	.248	.847	.186	.033	.168	.532	.383
NORTH CENTRAL	.236	.773	1.458	2.191	.897	.014	.157	.757	.138	.087	.154	.521	.355
East North Central	.233	.772	1.455	2.139	.905	.018	.164	.796	.142	.098	.164	.513	.363
West North Central	.238	.773	1.463	2.256	.882	.006	.141	.680	.128	.068	.135	.542	.340
SOUTH	.276	.741	1.371	1.903	.813	.044	.225	.911	.267	.137	.197	.519	.402
South Atlantic	.232	.718	1.324	1.885	.782	.049	.190	.864	.263	.179	.194	.496	.411
East South Central	.321	.775	1.407	1.810	.845	.045	.247	.974	.290	.066	.200	.619	.384
West South Central	.329	.749	1.416	2.044	.835	.039	.269	.961	.259	.100	.203	.616	.375
WEST	.267	.685	1.293	1.996	.825	.054	.235	.686	.226	.159	.158	.475	.328
Mountain	.236	.690	1.398	2.207	.849	.035	.215	.667	.195	.101	.137	.410	.303
Pacific	.289	.683	1.241	1.837	.812	.060	.241	.693	.237	.173	.166	.493	.336
NATIONAL (All Region Average)	.256	.737	1.371	2.007	.839	.034	.209	.818	.212	.121	.170	.512	.367

REGION	HIGH RISE				MOBILE HOMES				DUPLEX, TRIPLEX, QUADPLEX			
	Studio	1 BR	2 BR	Blended (All BRs)	1 BR	2 BR	3 BR	Blended (All BRs)	1 BR	2 BR	3 BR	Blended (All BRs)
NORTHEAST	.000	.004	.148	.035	.053	.182	.986	.483	.034	.269	.846	.423
New England	.000	.003	.066	.022	.000	.167	.917	.398	.020	.288	.824	.356
Middle Atlantic	.000	.004	.188	.041	.082	.188	1.005	.513	.044	.258	.854	.458
NORTH CENTRAL	.000	.000	.047	.011	.105	.193	.891	.475	.034	.202	.743	.310
East North Central	.000	.000	.058	.013	.096	.192	.961	.476	.045	.211	.748	.317
West North Central	.000	.013	.000	.004	.120	.194	.802	.474	.021	.184	.734	.299
SOUTH	.000	.017	.073	.041	.196	.249	.994	.551	.106	.276	.806	.419
South Atlantic	.000	.017	.073	.046	.191	.211	.986	.512	.102	.252	.809	.396
East South Central	.000	.000	.100	.021	.251	.312	.976	.589	.113	.318	.729	.440
West South Central	.000	.000	.000	.000	.176	.271	1.016	.586	.108	.292	.845	.444
WEST	.086	.052	.228	.132	.131	.166	.841	.416	.152	.277	.738	.397
Mountain	.000	.015	.000	.011	.159	.227	.881	.512	.082	.252	.652	.364
Pacific	.087	.061	.251	.150	.113	.131	.798	.347	.182	.288	.773	.412
NATIONAL (All Region Average)	.017	.011	.114	.045	.150	.213	.937	.497	.088	.257	.777	.387

Source: U.S. Department of Commerce, Bureau of the Census, *U.S. Census of Population and Housing* (Public Use Sample), 1980.

EXHIBIT 14

REGIONAL AND NATIONAL DEMOGRAPHIC MULTIPLIERS FOR *COMMON* CONFIGURATIONS OF *STANDARD* HOUSING TYPES FOR

SCHOOL-AGE CHILDREN (BY GRADE CATEGORY)

—BY HOUSING TYPE AND NUMBER OF BEDROOMS—
[For housing built during 1975-1980 and monitored in 1980]

REGION	GRADE	SINGLE FAMILY					GARDEN APARTMENTS				TOWNHOUSE			
		2 BR	3 BR	4 BR	5 BR	Blended (All BRs)	1 BR	2 BR	3 BR	Blended (All BRs)	1 BR	2 BR	3 BR	Blended (All BRs)
NORTHEAST	K6*	.134	.493	.814	.976	.530	.009	.154	.493	.108	.019	.103	.325	.223
	JHS*	.034	.138	.315	.526	.179	.003	.042	.212	.036	.010	.031	.126	.086
	HS*	.031	.103	.236	.454	.136	.005	.035	.152	.031	.010	.029	.099	.068
New England	K6	.175	.536	.845	.918	.526	.004	.136	.500	.097	.017	.074	.392	.186
	JHS	.037	.148	.343	.616	.176	.001	.034	.202	.030	.000	.012	.162	.074
	HS	.031	.109	.281	.517	.138	.002	.034	.181	.028	.035	.061	.122	.089
Middle Atlantic	K6	.103	.472	.803	.997	.532	.012	.165	.490	.114	.020	.111	.315	.231
	JHS	.032	.133	.305	.493	.180	.005	.046	.216	.039	.013	.037	.120	.089
	HS	.030	.100	.220	.431	.135	.006	.036	.141	.032	.000	.020	.096	.063
NORTH CENTRAL	K6	.148	.510	.828	1.046	.549	.007	.097	.451	.082	.068	.113	.288	.206
	JHS	.045	.149	.346	.594	.192	.003	.022	.164	.025	.005	.024	.123	.081
	HS	.042	.114	.284	.550	.156	.005	.037	.142	.031	.015	.017	.110	.068
East North Central	K6	.139	.511	.841	1.016	.559	.009	.100	.465	.084	.075	.125	.284	.215
	JHS	.047	.149	.340	.581	.193	.003	.023	.176	.026	.007	.024	.131	.085
	HS	.046	.112	.275	.543	.153	.006	.040	.155	.032	.015	.015	.098	.063
West North Central	K6	.159	.507	.805	1.085	.531	.002	.090	.423	.079	.055	.089	.296	.189
	JHS	.043	.148	.357	.611	.191	.002	.020	.140	.023	.000	.024	.106	.072
	HS	.037	.118	.301	.559	.160	.002	.031	.118	.027	.014	.022	.140	.079
SOUTH	K6	.179	.476	.775	.935	.497	.024	.150	.551	.164	.064	.125	.309	.232
	JHS	.057	.151	.320	.498	.176	.010	.040	.206	.056	.039	.042	.113	.093
	HS	.039	.114	.276	.470	.141	.010	.035	.154	.046	.034	.030	.097	.077
South Atlantic	K6	.148	.460	.757	.941	.476	.026	.125	.512	.159	.080	.123	.296	.236
	JHS	.046	.149	.304	.485	.170	.014	.035	.198	.058	.051	.039	.107	.094
	HS	.038	.109	.262	.460	.136	.009	.031	.154	.046	.048	.032	.093	.081
East South Central	K6	.215	.506	.787	.856	.522	.027	.176	.647	.192	.039	.114	.395	.223
	JHS	.071	.156	.334	.487	.182	.009	.039	.194	.056	.013	.050	.124	.083
	HS	.035	.113	.286	.466	.141	.009	.032	.133	.041	.013	.036	.100	.078
West South Central	K6	.214	.478	.792	1.000	.509	.020	.174	.567	.156	.050	.137	.350	.222
	JHS	.069	.150	.335	.542	.179	.007	.048	.226	.054	.030	.045	.141	.092
	HS	.046	.121	.288	.502	.147	.012	.046	.168	.049	.020	.021	.125	.061
WEST	K6	.174	.440	.748	1.069	.500	.032	.147	.401	.136	.102	.093	.268	.183
	JHS	.049	.132	.296	.485	.175	.008	.043	.151	.045	.036	.035	.100	.074
	HS	.044	.113	.249	.442	.150	.014	.045	.134	.045	.022	.030	.107	.071
Mountain	K6	.167	.460	.828	1.219	.531	.018	.142	.392	.120	.043	.075	.215	.157
	JHS	.036	.128	.312	.526	.174	.004	.038	.161	.039	.014	.031	.091	.075
	HS	.033	.102	.258	.461	.144	.013	.034	.114	.035	.043	.031	.104	.071
Pacific	K6	.179	.428	.709	.956	.483	.037	.149	.404	.142	.115	.099	.282	.191
	JHS	.059	.135	.288	.454	.176	.009	.044	.148	.047	.041	.036	.103	.074
	HS	.051	.119	.245	.427	.153	.014	.048	.141	.048	.017	.030	.108	.071
NATIONAL (All Region Average)	K6	.166	.479	.786	1.009	.513	.019	.135	.488	.129	.068	.108	.297	.211
	JHS	.050	.145	.319	.520	.180	.007	.036	.184	.043	.028	.034	.113	.084
	HS	.040	.113	.266	.478	.146	.009	.039	.146	.040	.024	.028	.102	.073

* K-6 encompasses kindergarten through 6th grade
JHS encompasses junior high school grades 7 through 9
HS encompasses high school grades 10 through 12

Source: U.S. Department of Commerce, Bureau of the Census, *U.S. Census of Population and Housing* (Public Use Sample), 1980.

EXHIBIT 14 (Continued)

REGIONAL AND NATIONAL DEMOGRAPHIC MULTIPLIERS FOR *COMMON* CONFIGURATIONS OF *STANDARD* HOUSING TYPES FOR

SCHOOL-AGE CHILDREN· (BY GRADE CATEGORY)

—BY HOUSING TYPE AND NUMBER OF BEDROOMS—
[For housing built during 1975-1980 and monitored in 1980]

REGION	GRADE	HIGH RISE				MOBILE HOMES				DUPLEX, TRIPLEX, QUADPLEX			
		Studio	1 BR	2 BR	Blended (All BRs)	1 BR	2 BR	3 BR	Blended (All BRs)	1 BR	2 BR	3 BR	Blended (All BRs)
NORTHEAST	K6*	.000	.003	.094	.020	.024	.109	.598	.289	.021	.179	.492	.254
	JHS*	.000	.001	.018	.006	.019	.042	.225	.113	.005	.045	.200	.092
	HS*	.000	.000	.036	.008	.010	.031	.162	.081	.008	.045	.154	.076
New England	K6	.000	.000	.033	.009	.000	.095	.566	.238	.012	.180	.473	.205
	JHS	.000	.003	.011	.009	.000	.037	.212	.092	.000	.051	.206	.077
	HS	.000	.000	.022	.004	.000	.035	.139	.068	.008	.057	.145	.075
Middle Atlantic	K6	.000	.004	.124	.025	.037	.114	.607	.307	.027	.178	.499	.280
	JHS	.000	.000	.021	.006	.030	.044	.229	.120	.008	.042	.198	.100
	HS	.000	.000	.043	.010	.015	.030	.168	.085	.008	.039	.157	.077
NORTH CENTRAL	K6	.000	.000	.030	.006	.058	.122	.540	.288	.018	.137	.438	.189
	JHS	.000	.000	.012	.002	.028	.034	.196	.102	.006	.031	.154	.061
	HS	.000	.000	.006	.003	.019	.037	.155	.085	.009	.034	.150	.061
East North Central	K6	.000	.000	.036	.008	.051	.119	.558	.278	.026	.142	.418	.190
	JHS	.000	.000	.014	.002	.029	.035	.228	.109	.006	.034	.165	.063
	HS	.000	.000	.007	.002	.015	.038	.176	.089	.012	.035	.165	.064
West North Central	K6	.000	.000	.000	.000	.070	.126	.518	.304	.009	.127	.476	.188
	JHS	.000	.000	.000	.000	.025	.032	.157	.092	.007	.025	.135	.056
	HS	.000	.000	.000	.004	.025	.036	.128	.079	.005	.032	.123	.055
SOUTH	K6	.000	.008	.030	.019	.130	.172	.622	.349	.061	.192	.502	.267
	JHS	.000	.002	.016	.010	.042	.045	.224	.120	.024	.046	.178	.087
	HS	.000	.002	.026	.013	.024	.032	.148	.081	.020	.038	.126	.064
South Atlantic	K6	.000	.011	.031	.021	.126	.144	.625	.325	.062	.169	.480	.248
	JHS	.000	.003	.017	.011	.042	.041	.224	.115	.022	.045	.185	.083
	HS	.000	.003	.025	.014	.023	.027	.136	.072	.018	.038	.144	.065
East South Central	K6	.000	.000	.000	.011	.173	.219	.606	.378	.056	.232	.470	.284
	JHS	.000	.000	.000	.005	.053	.055	.226	.128	.032	.047	.161	.090
	HS	.000	.000	.100	.005	.025	.038	.144	.083	.025	.038	.098	.066
West South Central	K6	.000	.000	.000	.000	.114	.189	.629	.369	.064	.207	.550	.290
	JHS	.000	.000	.000	.000	.037	.044	.221	.123	.023	.046	.179	.091
	HS	.000	.000	.000	.000	.025	.038	.166	.094	.021	.039	.116	.063
WEST	K6	.057	.034	.147	.074	.075	.101	.490	.242	.092	.170	.430	.240
	JHS	.000	.010	.046	.030	.030	.034	.200	.097	.031	.058	.159	.086
	HS	.029	.008	.035	.028	.026	.031	.150	.078	.029	.048	.150	.072
Mountain	K6	.000	.000	.000	.000	.091	.144	.527	.308	.047	.159	.390	.229
	JHS	.000	.000	.000	.000	.044	.046	.213	.119	.019	.048	.132	.071
	HS	.000	.015	.000	.011	.024	.037	.141	.086	.016	.046	.129	.063
Pacific	K6	.058	.041	.162	.085	.065	.076	.451	.194	.111	.175	.445	.244
	JHS	.000	.013	.050	.034	.020	.027	.186	.081	.036	.063	.170	.092
	HS	.029	.006	.039	.031	.027	.028	.161	.072	.035	.049	.158	.076
NATIONAL (All Region Average)	K6	.012	.007	.066	.024	.093	.140	.573	.306	.052	.170	.465	.239
	JHS	.000	.002	.021	.010	.034	.040	.213	.110	.019	.046	.170	.081
	HS	.006	.002	.027	.011	.023	.033	.151	.081	.017	.041	.142	.067

elementary school enrollments in the 1970s and secondary school enrollments in the 1980s. It will continue at both levels into the 1990s where it will impact on the number of high school graduates seeking higher education.

School-Age Children (Exhibit 13)

In 1980, school-age children per dwelling unit ranged from near zero in studio apartments to nearly two in a five-bedroom, single-family home. For comparable unit sizes (i.e., number of bedrooms), mobile homes, garden apartments, duplex/triplex/quadplex units and single-family homes produced the most school children; townhouses and high-rise units produced the least.

Taking into account the unit size types most often built, single-family homes by far produce the most school children and high-rise units produce the least.

Over the period 1970 to 1980 the number of school children per unit decreased, on average, at twice the percentage rate of the reduction in household size. School children per unit decreased by 30 percent; single family and garden apartments by 25 percent; high-rise and townhouse units by 40-50 percent. On the other hand, school-age children in mobile homes increased moderately over the decade across two of three bedroom configurations. This is particularly noticeable in western locations and especially along the West Coast (Pacific Region).

School-Age Children by Grade Category (Exhibit 14)

Generally speaking, across the larger (more bedrooms) housing types (single family and townhouses), the number of school children in elementary school (grades K-6) is 2-3 times more than the junior high and high school (grades 7-12). For the smaller-bedroom housing types (i.e., garden apartment and high rise), the number of school children in the elementary years approximately equals the sum of those in the junior high and high school years.

Public School-Age Children (Exhibits 15 and 16)

Using the Public Use Sample, it is possible to determine the average share of all students who attend public school as opposed to other sources of private education. In a fiscal impact analysis, this figure may be used to adjust downward the school-age children number to the pupil count impacting public services and expenditures. Public school enrollment projections would similarly factor the public school-age rather than total school-age children count to determine the anticipated future school population.

The percentage of all children attending public school by housing type varies between a low of 79 percent to a high of 96 percent. It is highest in the lower-value units such as mobile homes and garden apartments; it is lowest in higher-value units such as high rise, single-family homes, and townhouses.

An interesting aspect of public school attendance is that for most housing types, public school participation decreases with unit size. One explanation is that those who occupy larger, new housing units can afford to send a relatively larger share of their school-age children to private school.

For more expensive housing types, public school usage appears also to decrease with the age/grade of the student. It is highest in the lower grades where the public elementary school often is a reflection of neighborhood characteristics. As the grade increases and

EXHIBIT 15

REGIONAL AND NATIONAL DEMOGRAPHIC MULTIPLIERS FOR *COMMON* CONFIGURATIONS OF *STANDARD* HOUSING TYPES FOR

PERCENT OF SCHOOL-AGE CHILDREN IN PUBLIC SCHOOL

—BY HOUSING TYPE AND NUMBER OF BEDROOMS—
[For housing built during 1975-1980 and monitored in 1980]

REGION	SINGLE FAMILY 2 BR	3 BR	4 BR	5 BR	Blended (All BRs)	GARDEN APARTMENTS 1 BR	2 BR	3 BR	Blended (All BRs)	TOWNHOUSE 1 BR	2 BR	3 BR	Blended (All BRs)
NORTHEAST	91.92	89.64	87.30	84.61	88.36	94.29	90.88	88.97	91.53	100.00	87.61	87.92	88.25
New England	93.02	90.72	90.88	89.29	90.84	100.00	91.39	86.75	92.01	100.00	88.88	93.00	91.91
Middle Atlantic	90.59	89.04	85.82	82.81	87.14	93.16	90.60	89.81	91.33	100.00	87.35	86.95	87.51
NORTH CENTRAL	93.55	90.80	87.31	84.87	89.16	93.66	94.01	91.32	92.89	88.90	89.29	89.88	89.73
East North Central	92.50	90.37	86.28	81.72	88.36	95.60	93.35	88.96	91.71	92.32	87.86	90.39	89.78
West North Central	94.63	91.62	89.27	88.66	90.62	76.19	95.62	96.77	95.64	80.00	92.65	88.65	89.61
SOUTH	92.61	91.04	87.42	83.94	89.66	88.66	91.32	91.56	91.37	91.35	89.94	89.69	90.11
South Atlantic	90.41	90.31	86.36	84.10	88.65	87.73	91.60	90.12	90.51	89.27	88.37	90.29	90.22
East South Central	91.74	89.94	84.57	81.12	88.11	91.09	88.40	89.77	90.21	79.94	92.85	81.55	84.41
West South Central	95.90	92.55	90.33	86.11	91.84	88.69	92.64	94.97	93.28	100.00	93.27	90.87	92.72
WEST	92.18	93.20	91.45	91.11	92.20	94.23	93.87	92.66	93.37	94.85	89.56	91.56	91.89
Mountain	94.74	95.70	94.78	95.75	95.27	87.97	96.61	94.99	95.24	100.00	95.33	96.29	96.96
Pacific	90.73	91.79	89.62	86.87	90.40	95.37	93.08	91.89	92.83	94.10	87.73	90.45	90.39
NATIONAL (All Region Average)	92.59	91.23	88.37	86.52	89.95	91.84	92.65	91.60	92.25	92.71	89.37	89.92	90.29

REGION	HIGH RISE Studio	1 BR	2 BR	Blended (All BRs)	MOBILE HOMES 1 BR	2 BR	3 BR	Blended (All BRs)	DUPLEX, TRIPLEX, QUADPLEX 1 BR	2 BR	3 BR	Blended (All BRs)
NORTHEAST	—	100.00	82.91	83.29	100.00	95.95	95.77	95.90	66.76	82.86	84.88	82.23
New England	—	100.00	100.00	100.00	—	94.21	96.03	95.80	100.00	87.50	88.24	86.72
Middle Atlantic	—	100.00	79.97	79.61	100.00	96.49	95.71	95.94	56.24	80.02	83.69	80.41
NORTH CENTRAL	—	—	100.00	100.00	97.71	96.58	95.95	96.17	90.48	93.90	90.82	91.33
East North Central	—	—	100.00	100.00	100.00	96.83	96.27	96.49	91.03	92.80	91.30	91.23
West North Central	—	—	—	100.00	94.68	96.13	95.47	95.64	88.57	96.30	89.89	91.47
SOUTH	—	81.95	72.19	75.91	98.22	95.75	96.24	96.20	94.25	90.79	91.13	91.54
South Atlantic	—	81.98	71.43	74.24	98.48	95.70	96.24	96.19	93.24	89.10	88.97	89.82
East South Central	—	—	100.00	100.00	96.73	95.39	95.85	95.91	100.00	94.81	94.37	94.96
West South Central	—	—	—	—	98.81	96.12	96.49	96.40	92.15	90.55	92.41	92.00
WEST	100.00	75.05	71.10	75.02	95.58	96.10	97.50	97.19	92.37	93.57	94.54	93.63
Mountain	—	100.00	—	100.00	93.02	96.92	98.43	98.05	90.49	95.60	98.10	95.74
Pacific	100.00	73.64	71.12	74.72	97.88	95.27	96.40	96.28	92.74	92.77	93.35	92.82
NATIONAL (All Region Average)	100.00	80.00	76.92	78.71	97.26	95.96	96.42	96.40	91.56	91.71	91.16	91.06

Source: U.S. Department of Commerce, Bureau of the Census, *U.S. Census of Population and Housing* (Public Use Sample), 1980.

EXHIBIT 16

REGIONAL AND NATIONAL DEMOGRAPHIC MULTIPLIERS FOR *COMMON*
CONFIGURATIONS OF *STANDARD* HOUSING TYPES FOR

PERCENT OF CHILDREN IN PUBLIC SCHOOL BY GRADE

—BY HOUSING TYPE AND NUMBER OF BEDROOMS—
[For housing built during 1975-1980 and monitored in 1980]

REGION	GRADE	SINGLE FAMILY					GARDEN APARTMENTS				TOWNHOUSE			
		2 BR	3 BR	4 BR	5 BR	Blended (All BRs)	1 BR	2 BR	3 BR	Blended (All BRs)	1 BR	2 BR	3 BR	Blended (All BRs)
NORTHEAST	K6*	91.49	88.67	86.19	84.22	87.49	88.17	90.47	87.22	90.48	100.00	85.73	85.28	85.28
	JHS*	94.77	90.07	88.27	84.15	88.81	100.00	89.71	94.62	93.28	100.00	97.12	90.87	93.04
	HS*	90.58	93.69	89.85	85.94	91.05	100.00	94.05	86.77	93.20	100.00	84.35	92.85	91.91
New England	K6	92.74	90.28	91.27	92.02	90.86	100.00	93.16	85.10	92.60	100.00	94.44	96.56	94.20
	JHS	93.50	90.61	90.22	88.11	90.40	100.00	82.79	94.76	90.24	—	100.00	83.29	88.18
	HS	94.29	93.15	90.50	85.85	91.38	100.00	93.18	82.31	91.52	100.00	80.00	94.49	90.30
Middle Atlantic	K6	89.81	87.79	84.18	81.65	85.86	86.89	89.21	88.00	89.49	100.00	84.04	83.16	83.69
	JHS	95.69	89.77	87.43	82.39	88.06	100.00	92.69	94.53	94.37	100.00	96.74	92.36	94.04
	HS	88.08	93.99	89.50	85.96	90.92	100.00	94.21	88.88	94.14	—	88.12	92.60	92.42
NORTH CENTRAL	K6	92.32	89.39	84.95	82.80	87.58	93.94	93.92	91.20	92.83	85.74	88.86	90.09	89.83
	JHS	94.92	92.67	88.72	85.79	90.49	82.76	96.43	93.95	94.74	100.00	86.13	90.77	90.35
	HS	96.43	94.74	92.49	87.86	93.12	95.83	92.76	88.70	91.56	100.00	95.93	88.24	88.56
East North Central	K6	91.04	88.99	83.82	79.67	86.78	97.67	93.02	88.76	91.44	90.03	87.29	89.90	89.33
	JHS	94.95	92.10	88.02	82.49	89.75	93.94	95.73	91.46	93.77	100.00	83.61	91.19	89.91
	HS	94.40	94.45	91.66	84.75	92.37	96.77	92.79	86.78	90.77	100.00	100.00	90.66	91.00
West North Central	K6	93.51	90.14	87.24	86.50	89.06	79.17	96.12	96.52	96.06	75.00	93.38	90.58	90.98
	JHS	95.09	93.77	89.98	89.76	91.85	52.63	98.03	100.00	96.04	—	91.60	89.54	91.48
	HS	99.19	95.27	93.85	91.65	94.37	100.00	92.58	93.79	94.12	100.00	90.83	83.97	84.61
SOUTH	K6	91.12	89.25	85.18	80.22	87.84	86.97	89.37	90.11	89.82	86.82	88.71	88.80	89.07
	JHS	95.47	93.84	88.79	87.12	91.81	85.15	94.19	93 45	92.88	91.54	95.19	92.81	93.20
	HS	95.44	94.83	92.13	87.99	93.39	96.08	96.06	94.24	95.25	100.00	88.12	88.91	89.68
South Atlantic	K6	88.15	88.63	84.24	81.29	86.91	85.93	90.75	88.23	89.25	83.98	86.99	89.46	89.19
	JHS	94.60	92.69	87.71	86.39	90.67	88.24	9?.01	92.49	91.55	87.48	93.88	93.95	93.40
	HS	94.15	94.04	90.85	87.45	92.34	92.22	94.44	93.36	93.52	100.00	86.92	88.60	89.68
East South Central	K6	90.47	87.83	82.45	74.83	86.12	88.28	87.42	89.32	88.99	66.58	83.70	83.15	85.09
	JHS	94.50	93.71	85.97	86.46	90.89	100.00	89.57	88.17	91.28	100.00	92.80	80.78	85.92
	HS	94.24	94.25	88.82	87.08	91.82	90.91	92.43	94.21	94.44	100.00	89.92	76.20	80.79
West South Central	K6	95.18	90.87	87.88	82.34	90.04	87.88	89.04	93.70	91.05	100.00	91.39	88.33	90.77
	JHS	96.97	95.21	91.64	89.37	93.80	71.43	99.17	97.48	95.90	100.00	100.00	92.68	95.34
	HS	97.82	95.96	95.53	90.12	95.65	100.00	99.14	95.78	97.55	100.00	91.16	95.93	95.72
WEST	K6	91.55	91.84	89.91	89.82	90.86	93.12	93.55	92.04	92.87	94.69	89.54	90.47	90.85
	JHS	93.12	94.72	92.63	92.93	93.49	100.00	95.79	92.46	94.46	100.00	88.54	88.76	90.57
	HS	93.85	96.65	94.66	92.24	95.14	93.43	93.32	94.71	93.78	87.27	90.82	96.92	95.78
Mountain	K6	94.66	94.89	93.87	95.50	94.52	88.40	95.30	95.74	94.60	100.00	93.20	96.93	96.37
	JHS	94.71	97.19	95.80	95.75	96.21	100.00	98.44	91.37	95.43	100.00	100.00	95.28	98.13
	HS	95.21	97.56	96.51	96.47	96.88	83.33	100.00	97.54	97.18	100.00	96.13	95.07	96.09
Pacific	K6	89.60	90.01	87.64	84.31	88.60	93.80	93.01	90.80	92.30	94.10	88.54	89.09	89.37
	JHS	92.35	93.56	90.96	90.48	91.98	100.00	95.03	92.90	94.27	100.00	84.85	87.20	88.23
	HS	92.79	96.23	93.71	88.77	94.20	96.45	91.53	93.91	92.96	80.47	88.78	97.13	95.37
NATIONAL	K6	91.51	89.70	86.43	84.55	88.39	91.01	91.69	90.53	91.23	90.29	88.63	88.84	89.10
(All Region Average)	JHS	94.82	93.33	89.64	88.11	91.50	90.91	94.71	93.42	93.66	95.09	91.86	91.23	92.01
	HS	94.76	95.04	92.58	88.96	93.48	95.45	94.04	92.97	93.78	97.10	89.53	91.70	91.60

* K-6 encompasses kindergarten through 6th grade
JHS encompasses junior high school grades 7 through 9
HS encompasses high school grades 10 through 12

Source:　　U.S. Department of Commerce, Bureau of the Census, *U.S. Census of Population and Housing* (Public Use Sample), 1980.

EXHIBIT 16 (Continued)

REGIONAL AND NATIONAL DEMOGRAPHIC MULTIPLIERS FOR *COMMON* CONFIGURATIONS OF *STANDARD* HOUSING TYPES FOR

PERCENT OF CHILDREN IN PUBLIC SCHOOL BY GRADE

—BY HOUSING TYPE AND NUMBER OF BEDROOMS—
[For housing built during 1975-1980 and monitored in 1980]

REGION	GRADE	HIGH RISE Studio	1 BR	2 BR	Blended (All BRs)	MOBILE HOMES 1 BR	2 BR	3 BR	Blended (All BRs)	DUPLEX, TRIPLEX, QUADPLEX 1 BR	2 BR	3 BR	Blended (All BRs)
NORTHEAST	K6*	—	100.00	84.56	86.70	100.00	95.14	94.84	94.92	69.34	79.90	84.34	79.68
	JHS*	—	100.00	79.56	80.00	100.00	96.90	97.11	97.35	32.65	91.80	82.80	85.14
	HS*	—	—	80.06	76.47	100.00	97.14	97.35	97.52	79.27	85.81	89.36	87.19
New England	K6	—	—	100.00	100.00	—	93.26	94.15	94.21	100.00	84.32	87.18	85.54
	JHS	—	100.00	100.00	100.00	—	95.68	100.00	98.91	—	94.94	85.30	89.21
	HS	—	—	100.00	100.00	—	95.48	97.63	97.06	100.00	90.81	95.81	87.27
Middle Atlantic	K6	—	100.00	82.62	85.20	100.00	95.80	95.03	95.12	60.00	77.40	83.32	77.42
	JHS	—	—	74.88	66.07	100.00	97.27	96.42	96.93	33.73	89.66	81.80	83.43
	HS	—	—	75.12	72.55	100.00	98.00	97.27	97.54	66.27	81.65	87.16	87.34
NORTH CENTRAL	K6	—	—	100.00	100.00	96.04	95.72	95.46	95.59	100.00	93.12	87.89	89.68
	JHS	—	—	100.00	100.00	100.00	98.24	96.69	96.97	83.08	98.07	96.50	95.39
	HS	—	—	100.00	100.00	100.00	97.85	96.71	97.18	74.71	93.24	93.47	92.42
East North Central	K6	—	—	100.00	100.00	100.00	96.23	95.97	96.22	100.00	92.17	88.07	89.51
	JHS	—	—	100.00	100.00	100.00	98.57	96.62	96.79	67.21	97.67	95.81	94.78
	HS	—	—	100.00	100.00	100.00	97.11	96.70	96.96	82.79	91.09	94.96	92.98
West North Central	K6	—	—	—	—	90.95	94.91	94.76	94.70	100.00	95.26	87.64	89.99
	JHS	—	—	—	—	100.00	98.45	96.68	97.27	100.00	100.00	98.15	96.45
	HS	—	—	—	100.00	100.00	98.60	96.87	97.47	48.94	97.54	89.58	91.26
SOUTH	K6	—	85.71	66.78	74.73	97.31	95.01	95.44	95.48	91.22	89.20	90.51	90.53
	JHS	—	100.00	75.31	86.87	100.00	96.41	97.90	97.33	100.00	94.57	93.32	93.90
	HS	—	50.00	76.89	68.25	100.00	98.46	97.09	97.54	96.55	93.96	90.53	92.71
South Atlantic	K6	—	85.45	66.67	72.82	97.70	94.65	95.49	95.42	91.14	87.69	88.32	88.81
	JHS	—	100.00	75.00	85.59	100.00	97.54	97.77	97.39	100.00	92.31	91.72	92.46
	HS	—	51.61	75.00	66.90	100.00	98.51	97.28	97.79	92.74	91.76	87.63	90.26
East South Central	K6	—	—	—	100.00	95.25	94.56	94.72	94.84	100.00	92.90	94.64	94.36
	JHS	—	—	—	100.00	100.00	96.54	97.92	97.81	100.00	100.00	96.08	97.22
	HS	—	—	100.00	100.00	100.00	98.44	97.37	97.94	100.00	100.00	90.29	94.44
West South Central	K6	—	—	—	—	98.16	95.81	95.84	95.94	86.66	88.84	91.17	90.65
	JHS	—	—	—	—	100.00	95.22	98.05	97.15	100.00	95.25	94.18	93.84
	HS	—	—	—	—	100.00	98.69	96.86	97.24	100.00	94.09	95.53	95.56
WEST	K6	100.00	61.58	75.88	73.51	94.29	95.06	96.76	96.28	91.07	92.13	92.44	92.03
	JHS	—	100.00	55.58	75.00	94.95	98.22	98.75	98.55	92.36	96.92	97.36	95.44
	HS	100.00	100.00	71.55	78.95	100.00	97.78	98.27	98.46	96.21	94.80	97.66	96.54
Mountain	K6	—	—	—	—	91.83	96.12	98.01	97.53	83.37	94.83	98.10	94.68
	JHS	—	—	—	—	91.67	98.47	99.44	98.99	100.00	98.32	98.18	98.03
	HS	—	100.00	— ·	100.00	100.00	98.12	98.58	98.72	100.00	95.02	98.07	97.00
Pacific	K6	100.00	61.69	75.86	73.52	96.34	93.82	95.21	94.90	92.59	91.05	90.48	90.99
	JHS	—	100.00	55.47	75.07	100.00	97.76	97.90	98.01	90.93	96.37	97.11	94.67
	HS	100.00	100.00	71.36	77.81	100.00	97.16	98.13	98.20	95.39	94.49	97.53	96.58
NATIONAL	K6	100.00	73.61	78.64	79.17	96.22	95.15	95.67	95.62	90.50	90.18	89.63	89.62
(All Region Average)	JHS	—	100.00	71.09	80.61	98.24	97.23	97.79	97.64	93.01	95.89	93.47	93.56
	HS	100.00	81.25	77.29	76.11	100.00	97.89	97.35	97.78	93.14	93.38	93.31	93.15

there is more chance for regionalization and also as the stakes increase for college entry, private education is more frequently sought. For less-expensive housing types, and most specifically mobile homes, the reverse is true. The percentage of those who attend public schools is initially high and further increases in the high school years. Costs for secondary private education are much higher than the costs for elementary education.

Pre-School Children (Exhibit 17)

Pre-school children are an increasing concern in certain types of fiscal impact studies. This is especially true when the analysis involves future school district enrollment projections. The standard type of enrollment projection uses a cohort survival technique wherein information on children aged 0 to 5—pre-school children—is of prime importance for determining future kindergarten enrollment.

Pre-school children for the larger-bedroom housing types (single-family homes and townhouses) are one-quarter to one-half the level of school-age children for these housing types. For the smaller-bedroom housing types and for mobile homes, pre-school children are on a par with school-age children. In mobile homes, the absolute level of pre-school children is higher than that for garden apartments and high-rise units. Interestingly, in one-bedroom garden apartments, the number of pre-school children actually exceeds by a moderate factor the number of school-age children for the dwelling type.

A CONCLUDING STATEMENT ABOUT MULTIPLIERS

Demographic multipliers have been used in fiscal impact analysis for nearly two decades. Beginning with field survey and moving to the data of the *Census of Population and Housing* and then to the *American (Annual) Housing Survey,* we have become increasingly sophisticated in both the definition of housing types and the specification of who and how many people live in dwelling units of various kinds and sizes.

Housing-unit size continues to be the dominant criterion affecting both household size and school-age children. Thus many more people and enhanced school loads are found in units of three rather than two bedrooms across all housing types. This is opposed to much less significant differences in the number of occupants found in the same bedroom configuration of single-family homes versus garden apartments, versus townhouses, etc.

Less-expensive, larger units of rental tenure usually have more people and school children than more-expensive, equivalent-size units of ownership tenure. Thus, three-bedroom garden apartments or mobile homes usually have considerably more occupants than three-bedroom, single-family homes or townhouses. Smaller units and especially small, expensive units have the fewest occupants of all.

There has been a two-decade trend downward of both household size and school-age children by dwelling type. This has not happened to the same degree in all dwelling types. Mobile homes and larger garden apartments may actually show slight increases in household size (and school children) over time.

The trend in household size reduction seems to have stabilized at the present time, but for most dwelling types there has not been a swing in the opposite direction despite the baby-boom echo (children of the baby-boom generation).

The continued trend toward small households has caused some difficulty in the use of U.S. Census versus field-survey multipliers. Census multipliers appear to be consistently higher than the number of school children found on-site by field survey immediately after development occupancy. U.S. Census pre-school children counts are only slightly larger than what is observed in field survey; thus, initial aging of the new development population would appear not to account for the field/Census difference in household size and school-age children.

EXHIBIT 17

REGIONAL AND NATIONAL DEMOGRAPHIC MULTIPLIERS FOR *COMMON* CONFIGURATIONS OF *STANDARD* HOUSING TYPES FOR

PRE-SCHOOL CHILDREN

—BY HOUSING TYPE AND NUMBER OF BEDROOMS—

[For housing built during 1975-1980 and monitored in 1980]

| REGION | SINGLE FAMILY | | | | | GARDEN APARTMENTS | | | | TOWNHOUSE | | | |
	2 BR	3 BR	4 BR	5 BR	Blended (All BRs)	1 BR	2 BR	3 BR	Blended (All BRs)	1 BR	2 BR	3 BR	Blended (All BRs)
NORTHEAST	.194	.427	.374	.291	.368	.025	.168	.393	.108	.053	.112	.266	.181
New England	.233	.414	.355	.228	.352	.010	.167	.202	.087	.017	.107	.203	.123
Middle Atlantic	.165	.433	.381	.313	.377	.034	.168	.463	.120	.066	.114	.275	.193
NORTH CENTRAL	.240	.436	.386	.371	.395	.026	.175	.337	.119	.044	.148	.241	.181
East North Central	.204	.427	.387	.364	.390	.027	.170	.293	.114	.068	.148	.257	.195
West North Central	.282	.451	.384	.379	.404	.024	.185	.423	.129	.000	.148	.204	.152
SOUTH	.189	.337	.286	.258	.304	.046	.178	.324	.149	.087	.154	.220	.185
South Atlantic	.142	.303	.263	.257	.268	.039	.146	.269	.129	.073	.131	.227	.185
East South Central	.270	.389	.299	.247	.354	.042	.198	.396	.167	.079	.229	.186	.188
West South Central	.225	.347	.310	.274	.324	.055	.222	.385	.166	.110	.192	.192	.181
WEST	.243	.376	.368	.444	.354	.062	.203	.319	.161	.102	.099	.154	.127
Mountain	.326	.463	.452	.581	.440	.038	.205	.353	.152	.058	.056	.169	.103
Pacific	.185	.327	.326	.339	.306	.071	.202	.307	.164	.112	.116	.150	.135
NATIONAL (All Region Average)	.213	.377	.343	.348	.344	.041	.183	.330	.140	.079	.128	.212	.165

| | HIGH RISE | | | | MOBILE HOMES | | | | DUPLEX, TRIPLEX, QUADPLEX | | | |
	Studio	1 BR	2 BR	Blended (All BRs)	1 BR	2 BR	3 BR	Blended (All BRs)	1 BR	2 BR	3 BR	Blended (All BRs)
NORTHEAST	.000	.001	.083	.016	.067	.203	.486	.297	.042	.236	.334	.220
New England	.000	.000	.044	.009	.013	.122	.417	.203	.020	.247	.351	.201
Middle Atlantic	.000	.001	.102	.018	.097	.234	.505	.329	.058	.230	.328	.230
NORTH CENTRAL	.000	.000	.071	.011	.144	.271	.502	.355	.066	.219	.265	.202
East North Central	.000	.000	.079	.013	.121	.267	.469	.332	.081	.210	.260	.201
West North Central	.000	.000	.033	.004	.183	.279	.545	.393	.049	.235	.274	.204
SOUTH	.000	.006	.026	.013	.192	.304	.470	.359	.133	.216	.313	.225
South Atlantic	.000	.008	.021	.012	.131	.249	.447	.313	.105	.185	.289	.197
East South Central	.000	.000	.100	.016	.288	.392	.492	.427	.137	.251	.404	.265
West South Central	.000	.000	.286	.036	.232	.335	.487	.388	.174	.249	.295	.247
WEST	.029	.055	.107	.069	.127	.162	.460	.261	.180	.262	.302	.274
Mountain	.000	.000	.000	.000	.176	.250	.540	.363	.125	.314	.353	.317
Pacific	.029	.067	.117	.079	.095	.111	.372	.186	.203	.238	.282	.255
NATIONAL (All Region Average)	.006	.008	.061	.021	.152	.254	.475	.329	.113	.233	.301	.234

Source: U.S. Department of Commerce, Bureau of the Census, *U.S. Census of Population and Housing* (Public Use Sample), 1980.

There is another explanation, however. There is almost a ten-year lag in some of the data (i.e., units built 1975 to 1980, monitored in 1980 by the Census, versus field surveys in 1985). Clearly, the age of the Census data is having an effect on its usefulness for impact purposes. U.S. Census numbers, in practice, are now being used as the *upper* limits of predicted school children and household-size demand estimates.